T0102307

VEDANTA
and
CHRISTIAN FAITH

VEDANTA
and
CHRISTIAN FAITH

BEDE GRIFFITHS

FOREWORD BY
CYPRIAN CONSIGLIO, OSB CAM.

MONKFISH BOOK PUBLISHING COMPANY
RHINEBECK, NEW YORK

Vedanta and Christian Faith Copyright © 1973, 2023 by Bede Griffiths

All rights reserved. No part of this book may be used or reproduced in any manner without the consent of the publisher except in critical articles or reviews. Contact the publisher for information.

Paperback ISBN 978-1-958972-16-8
eBook ISBN 978-1-958972-17-5

Library of Congress Cataloging-in-Publication Data

Names: Griffiths, Bede, 1906-1993, author. | Consiglio, Cyprian, writer of
 foreword.
Title: Vedanta and Christian faith / Bede Griffiths ; foreword by Cyprian
 Consiglio, OSB.
Description: Rhinebeck, New York : Monkfish Book Publishing Company, [2023]
Identifiers: LCCN 2023011199 (print) | LCCN 2023011200 (ebook) | ISBN
 9781958972168 (paperback) | ISBN 9781958972175 (ebook)
Subjects: LCSH: Christianity and other religions--Hinduism. |
 Hinduism--Relations--Christianity. | Vedanta.
Classification: LCC BR128.H5 G75 2023 (print) | LCC BR128.H5 (ebook) |
 DDC 261.2/45--dc23/eng/20231107
LC record available at https://lccn.loc.gov/2023011199
LC ebook record available at https://lccn.loc.gov/2023011200

Book and cover design by Colin Rolfe

Monkfish Book Publishing Company
22 East Market Street, Suite 304
Rhinebeck, New York 12572
(845) 876-4861
monkfishpublishing.com

CONTENTS

FOREWORD

CYPRIAN CONSIGLIO, OSB

THOSE OF US WHO ARE students of the thought of Bede Griffiths, and others of us who consider ourselves to be in his lineage, are pleased with any resurgence of interest in his life, his work, and especially his thought. And so, we are grateful to welcome this republication of *Vedanta and Christian Faith*.

This is a relatively early book in Fr. Bede's oeuvre and is probably the least-known. It was first published in 1973, before the series of his best-known books first published in the US by Templegate, beginning in 1976 with *Return to the Center*. Besides the four works for Templegate, there were three major titles for other publishing houses as well. All that to say, the thought in *Vedanta and Christian Faith*, Bede's "voice" you might say, has both a tone and a content decidedly different from his later voice.

I am most tempted to contrast it to *New Creation in Christ*, for example (1992, Darton, Longman &

Todd). That book is a series of lectures "on Christian Meditation and Community" for the John Main seminar, a series that inspired the founding of the World Community for Christian Meditation, and in it you hear Bede's most mature voice. He speaks with the authority of experience, nearly 60 years a monk, over half of those in India, steeped in classical Scholastic theology and Gregorian liturgy as well as in the various Indian darshanas and the beloved Sanskrit chants and inculturated Indian rituals. In *New Creation*, Bede is not speaking now from the West/Europe and now from the East/Asia. His thought is seamless, as if there were only one philosophy, the perennial philosophy, the universal wisdom. (The last works of the late Irish Jesuit William Johnston (1925-2010), another teacher of mysticism and meditation, were like that as well. Johnston was based in Japan and an expert in Buddhist-Christian dialogue.)

The three lectures that make up *Vedanta and Christian Faith*, on the other hand, are Bede's "first substantial draft of a synthesis of the two worlds of Hinduism and Christianity." That is how Bruno Barnhart, who edited the definitive collection of Bede's principal works in the masterfully annotated *The One Light*, described it. Here we see Bede rigorous in his distinctions, and careful in his insistence on working from "the orthodox tradition" of both Hinduism and Christianity where, he says, "the most profound thought is to be found."

What Bede does not mention in his brief autobiographical notes at the end of the preface is that his Oxford years were spent under the tutelage of C.S. Lewis. And as I read his explication of the "orthodox tradition of each religion" I could imagine him having similar discussions in Lewis' rooms, an interlocuter who would not have let an empty phrase nor a slip of logic pass unchallenged. (Some of his intellectual sparring with Lewis continued into Bede's early years in India, as evidenced by some of Lewis' letters to him preserved in the archives at the Graduate Theological Union in Berkeley, CA. Lewis was not totally convinced of his former student and friend's launch into the world of inter-religiosity.)

The philosophy of the Vedanta, at least in our present era, is not completely foreign to almost anyone who has delved at all into contemporary inter-religious (or "interspiritual") dialogue. Bede does not go far into explaining, perhaps assuming pre-knowledge, what Vedanta is. The Sanskrit word *vedānta* literally means the 'end' (Sk. *anta*) of the Vedas or the Vedic Period. The four Vedas—the Rig, Sama, Yashur and Atharva Vedas—may come from a period as early as the 13th century BCE with the later ones written as recent as the 4th century BCE. They contain hymns to the gods and, since sacrifice was thought to be the center of religion, also a plethora of details about and formulas for sacrifices and rituals, oracles, charms and even what might strike us as magic spells. The Vedas also contain some commentaries on the meaning of the sacrifices along with a bit of philosophical and theological doctrine.

Attached to each of the Vedas, however, are various *upanishads*, a word that means 'sitting close by devotedly.' The Upanishads are records of sessions between spiritual masters and their disciples, dealing not with rituals, sacrifices and hymns but rather with the inner journey to discover the ground of being-*brahman* which is one with the ground of consciousness-*atman*, a reality which rituals cannot reach but which underlies all of life. This reality "is the essence of every created thing, and the same Reality as our real Self, so that each one of us is one with the power that created and sustains the universe."[1] This discovery of the *rishis* ('seers') of the Upanishads marks a seminal point in the development of the Indian spiritual evolution. Even saying that much barely touches the depth of this experience and at the same time is already saying too much, for it is indeed an experience that must be had, not an abstract philosophical thought to grasp. Bede himself would write later in *Marriage of East and West* about the intuition of the Upanishads that

It is basic to all human experience, it is the ultimate truth; it is 'that which being known everything is known.' It was discovered by the seers of the Upanishads and has been passed down in India from generation to generation; in it is contained the 'wisdom' of India. It has been

known in other religions too, in the traditions of
Buddhism and Taoism and in the mystical tradition of Islam.[2]

The Vedanta then is the systematic philosophy or
philosophies that draw a metaphysics from out of this
experience. One could hazard to say that the *Advaita
Vedanta* of the eight-century wandering sage philosopher Shankara is the best known of the philosophies
to be drawn from the Upanishads, *ad-vaita* meaning literally 'not two,' that is, the human self and the
Ultimate Self (God, *Brahman, Atman, Purusha*) are
not two. The famous image that captures this experience is that the individual self (*jivātman*) disappears
into the great Self (*paramatman*) like a drop into
the ocean. But here you will see Bede digs further
into alternate philosophical expressions of the ramifications of this spiritual experience and intuition,
the so-called "qualified non-duality" or *Visis-advaita*
of the 11th century Ramanuja and the 13th century
Dvaita-vedanta school of thought of Madhva. Bede's
own preference lies somewhat closest to Ramanuja.

Just as the Indian spiritual genius needed a philosophical language to express its ramifications in
practical intellectual terms (hence the Vedanta), so
too the first catechists of the Christian biblical revelation leaned immediately on the Greek tradition,
of Plato first but then of Aristotle and the Neo-
Platonists, to express the meaning of the Christ
event. Many of them are cited by Bede here. The

difference is that the Vedanta grew *out of* the intuitive experience of the Upanishads, whereas the philosophy of Plato and Aristotle *preceded* Christianity, new wine poured into old wineskins.

Late intertestamental Judaism, especially of the diaspora in North Africa, was heavily influenced by Hellenistic thought and culture, including the Deuterocanonical books which were either written in Greek such as the Wisdom of Solomon or known only by their Greek version such as Sirach. For that reason, some think that the marriage of Greek thought to Christian revelation was providential. However, one of the innovations of Catholic thought after the Second Vatican Council was to permit and even encourage re-articulating the kerygma using new philosophical language. And part of recognizing that Christianity had become a world church rather than a Western European export was breaking out even of our Roman-Greek Eurocentric philosophy. As Raimon Panikkar put it, "If Christ is to have any meaning for Hindus, Andines, Ibos, Vietnamese, and others who do not belong to the Abrahamic lineage, this meaning can no longer be offered in the garb of Western philosophies."[3] Some such as Bruno Barnhart would go so far as to suggest that the "crystalline Greek theology" had actually "arrested the historical and affective *dynamism* that is intrinsic to Christianity."[4] Is this why Bede says at the end of that same passage quoted above that though the intuition of the Upanishads has also "been present in Christianity from the beginning, and is the inner secret of the Gospel ... it has often been obscured, and today in the West it has almost been lost."[5] Bede too grew to find Greek terms often too confining, especially the tendency toward a dualism between spirit and matter, and in the way Greek thought subordinates and even excludes *psyche* and the feminine dimension of the human person.

What thinkers such as Bede Griffiths asked was what if Christianity could be interpreted and passed on using the language of the Vedanta, or the language of Mahayana Buddhism, or the language of Taoism? And if not then, why not now? Is it possible to take our experience of the gospel and our tradition, and try to articulate them using other philosophical or mystical languages? This really is the central question that leads into this work. Bede and his predecessors at Shantivanam, Jules Monchanin (1895-1957) and Abhishiktananda (Henri le Saux, OSB, 1910-1973), along with other pioneers of Hindu-Christian dialogue, thought that this may have been the reason for the failure of missionary efforts in the Orient, especially in India, because Christianity used a philosophical language that makes little sense to the Asian mind. The Church so often tried to pass on Greek terms and Roman culture (hence Plato and Aristotle, the Roman Rite of the Mass and Gregorian chant) instead of allowing the seed of the kerygma to take root in the soil of native philosophical and cultural genius, allowing that the spark of the Divine, the 'seeds of the Word,' and the inspiration of the Holy Spirit had already been at work in other traditions as well.

It's good to keep this in mind, that *Vedanta and Christian Faith* was written not even a decade after *Nostra Aetate*, the ground-breaking 1965 document of the Catholic Church that brought about an official reversal of the Church's position "On the Relation of the Church to Non-Christian Religions." Bede Griffiths was uniquely placed in his area of expertise, along with many of the theologians of the so-called *nouvelle theologie* in the early 20th century, to anticipate and prepare for the work of Vatican II, however unknowingly, by delving into areas of research that were not only suspect in the Counter-Reformation atmosphere of the Roman Catholic Church, but at times downright condemned, such as interreligious, even simply ecumenical, dialogue. Bede's move to India in 1955, well before the idea of an ecumenical council was even in the air, gave him an authority and a solid foundation. His keen intellect and stellar academic background, coupled with his voracious spiritual hunger, afforded him the means to sketch this "synthesis of the two worlds of Hinduism and Christianity." Even if it is merely a draft, he does it with aplomb and elegance.

Cyprian Consiglio, OSB Cam.

New Camaldoli Hermitage
Big Sur, CA

AUTHOR'S PREFACE

THE DIFFERENT RELIGIONS of the world grew up in isolation from one another and were often engaged in conflict, but today they are meeting in a way which has never taken place before. It is no longer possible for one religion to isolate itself from another. It is no longer possible to be a mature Christian without taking into account the other religions of the world, just as it is no longer possible to be a mature Hindu or Buddhist without taking account of Christianity. This means that the different religions have now to enter into dialogue with one another. It is no longer a question of a Christian going about to convert others to his faith, but of each one being ready to listen to the other and so to grow together in mutual understanding. The situation between the different religions of the world is like that between the different Christian churches. The different churches do not now seek to convert Christians from one church to another, but rather to grow together as churches in the knowledge of

Christ and his will for the Church and so to work towards Christian unity. So also with the different religions of the world. The divine Mystery, the eternal Truth, has been revealing itself to all men from the beginning of history. Every people has received some insight into this divine mystery—which is the mystery of human existence—and every religion, from the most primitive to the most advanced, has its own unique insight into the one Truth. These insights, insofar as they each reflect the one Reality, are in principle complementary. Each has its own defects both of faith and practice, and each has to learn from others, so they may grow together to that unity in Truth which is the goal of human existence. In this process no religion is required to give up the essential Truth by which it lives, but each may be required to give up many accidental elements which have entered into it in the course of history. One may believe that humanity is slowly evolving towards an ultimate unity of religion in which God will be worshipped in Spirit and in Truth, but this is still only on the horizon, and meanwhile we have to work towards a mutual understanding and appreciation of the different religious traditions. These lectures are an attempt to see the Christian faith in the light of Vedanta as a result of eighteen years lived in India, in contact with the living faiths of India. The aim has been to set the orthodox tradition of the Christian faith alongside the orthodox tradition of the Vedanta and to see how they can mutually enrich one another. It is by such mutuality, wherein each religion is contacted at the deepest level of its experience of God, that one may hope the growth towards unity may best be achieved, and it is towards this end that these lectures are directed.

As regards the facts of my life, I was born on December 17, 1906, in England and was educated at Christ's Hospital school (where Coleridge and Charles Lamb were also educated) and at Magdalen College, Oxford. After leaving Oxford I joined with two friends in leading a life of extreme simplicity in a Cotswold village, when I began to read the Bible and other Christian literature seriously. At Oxford I had given up the practice of any religion, but this experience in the country led me to a new understanding of Christianity, and I was eventually received into the Catholic Church and became a Benedictine monk.

My interest in Indian thought was awakened even before I became a Catholic, but I began the serious study of Indian thought, both Hindu and Buddhist, soon after I was ordained a priest in 1940. Soon after this I met an Indian monk and with him came to India where I have been living for the last eighteen years. I lived for twelve years in Kerala, where I joined in founding a monastery in the Syrian rite, and since then I have been living here in the Tamil Nadu in an ashram founded in 1950, which is dedicated to the reconciliation of Indian and Christian thought under the conditions of life of a Hindu ashram. We aim at creating a center where people of different religious traditions can meet together in an atmosphere of prayer and learn to grow together towards that unity in Truth which is the goal of all religion.

Bede Griffiths

Shantivanam
South India
May 21, 1973

VEDANTA
and
CHRISTIAN FAITH

I. THE MYSTERY OF THE GODHEAD

Hinduism and Christianity are two religions which grew up until recently in complete independence of one another. Each religion has been engaged over a period of four thousand years (if we include the Judaic origin of Christianity) in a continuous quest for a right understanding of the nature of God, the Supreme Being, and of man's relation to him. Each religion has evolved an elaborate system of theology, in which this understanding of the nature of God and of man has been worked out on a rational basis and these two systems may well be considered to be the most profound penetration into the ultimate nature of reality which the world has seen. Yet, though many Christians have in modern times been influenced by Hinduism and many Hindus by Christianity, very little attempt has been made so far to compare the orthodox tradition of Hinduism with the orthodox tradition of Christianity. Most commonly it has been the unorthodox in each religion who have felt the attraction of the other, and who have attempted to combine elements from each religion in a new synthesis. Yet it is in the orthodox tradition of a religion that its most profound thought is to be found, and it is in the attempt to compare the deepest insights of orthodox tradition in each religion that we are most likely to approach the ultimate truth.

By the orthodox tradition of Hinduism I mean the Vedanta and by the orthodox tradition of Christianity I mean the theological tradition, which was common to both Eastern and Western Christendom for over a thousand years and which still remains the basis of Christian orthodoxy. The Vedanta is the system of philosophy which has grown up from the original revelation of the Vedas and constitutes, as its name implies, the "end" of the Vedas. The properly philosophical doctrine was first developed in the Upanishads in the sixth century before Christ, and the tradition has grown up over the succeeding centuries, being enriched by many currents from different sources, above all the current of *bhakti*, or devotion to a personal God, which gave us the Bhagavad Gita. It has developed various systems of philosophy, notably the *Advaita*, or non-dualist, doctrine of Sankara (9th c), the *Visishtad-vaita*, or qualified nondualism, of Ramanuja (11th c), and the *Dvaita*, or dualism, of Madhva (13th c). Still today all these systems have their adherents, and what is more, new interpretations of the Vedanta in the light of modern thought have been attempted like that of Sri Aurobindo of Pondicherry, who has created a new system of Vedanta, based on an evolutionary view of life. Thus the Vedanta presents us with a complex system of thought, which has grown up over three thousand years and is still alive at the present day.

Christian theology has had a similar history. Based on the original revelation of the Bible, which derives from the first millenium before Christ, it was developed through contact with Greek thought by the Greek and Latin Fathers of the Church and elaborated into different systems of theology, Platonic and Aristotelian, in the Middle Ages, notably by St. Thomas Aquinas and St. Bonaventure and Duns Scotus. Though suffering an eclipse to some extent in the succeeding centuries, it has been revived again in our own time and seeks to renew itself by contact with modern thought. The question which I want to raise in these lectures is: Cannot these two systems of thought, that of the Vedanta and that of Christian faith, meet and enrich one another? Can the Vedanta learn from Christian faith, as it has learned from the different currents of Saivite and Vaishnavite faith, which it has encountered in the course of its history, and so develop along new lines? And can the Christian faith, which first elaborated its philosophy through contact with Greek thought, be brought now into vital contact with the Vedanta, and so develop a new system of philosophy and discover new implications of doctrine? It is my belief that the time has come for such a meeting to take place. Both Hinduism and Christianity are being forced to reconsider their philosophy in the light of modern science and secular philosophy. May it not be that the challenge of modern science and secularism may enable both religions to come to a deeper understanding of the implications of their faith and to find an answer to the problems which face the modern world? These problems I propose to divide into three—the problem of the existence and nature of God, or the ultimate reality; the problem of creation and the relation of man and the universe to this ultimate truth; and finally the problem of the ultimate state of man and the universe.

It is well known that a crisis has arisen in the West over the problem of the existence of God. The "death of God," which was proclaimed by Nietzsche in the last century, has now been accepted as a fact by a large part of Europe and America and has become a matter of concern for Christian theologians. What this means is that the image and concept of God, which has prevailed in Western Europe over the past two thousand years, has apparently lost its meaning and relevance. What is the reason for this? It is due, no doubt, to a complex process of psychological development, but one of the basic reasons for this is that the original Hebrew revelation of God was given in largely anthropomorphic terms. The Hebrew conceived of God as above all a Person, a moral Being, who is known by his action in history, his providence over the life both of nations and of individuals. It is true that he was forbidden to form any image of God and conceived of him as a "hidden God," dwelling in cloud and darkness; but he never hesitated to speak of him in human terms, ascribing to him human passions, of anger and repentance, of love and desire, of hatred and revenge, of joy and sorrow. Unfortunately the Hebrew had no power of metaphysical thought—he thought in images, not in concepts—so that this representation of God, which is legitimate if it is properly understood, was never analyzed philosophically. Even the Christian conception of God in the New Testament suffered from this defect. The idea of God as a "Father in heaven" is deeply significant, but its significance has to be worked out philosophically, and the idea of an incarnation of God, of God revealing himself in the form of a man, has tended to strengthen the habit of thinking of God in anthropomorphic terms.

As a result, where the Bible has been accepted as the final form of Christian revelation, an essentially unphilosophical image of God has tended to prevail. The Greek Fathers of the Church, however, who inherited the metaphysical mind of the Greeks, were able to correct this tendency. To them we owe the formation of an adequate philosophical conception of God, in so far as he can be conceived by the human mind. Beginning with the Apologists, Justin and Athenagoras in the second century, and continuing through the Greek and Latin Fathers, especially St. Gregory of Nyssa and St. Augustine, under the influence of Plato, the Church gradually achieved a masterly conception of the divine nature in the work of St. Thomas Aquinas, who built on the tradition of the Bible and the Fathers, using the philosophical method of Aristotle. The conception of God, which was formulated by St. Thomas Aquinas, is in my opinion the most adequate which the human mind has been able to achieve. But even this conception has now come under attack. This is due partly to a prejudice against all metaphysical thought, which the scientific mind tends to produce, but more seriously to the fact that the metaphysical conception of God always tends to be mistaken for the reality, and the concept of God becomes an "idol" no less than the image. But, in fact, all language about God, as Aquinas himself well understood, is necessarily analogical. We cannot speak one word properly about God; even to say that God "exists" is to speak in terms of analogy, since God's mode of existence is totally different from that of any other being. Of God we can only say what he is not; what he is can never properly be said.

Thus it is not only the image of God but also the metaphysical concept which has broken down for modern man. We are faced with the ultimate mystery of God before which speech and thought are silent. Now it is here that it seems to me that India has something to say to modern man. India has never been so preoccupied with images and concepts of God as has Western man. In India it was understood from the beginning that God cannot properly be imagined or conceived. To my mind this is the supreme achievement of India that at the very beginning of her history she was able to break through the veil, not only of the senses but also of the intellect, and to discover the hidden mystery which lies beyond speech and thought. This discovery was made in the sixth century before Christ by Gautama Buddha and the seers of the Upanishads. The Buddha's conception of *Nirvana* is essentially that of a state which transcends both speech and thought. It is that which is known when the light of this world is "blown out," when desire ceases, when thought ceases, when all "becoming" ceases. It is the ultimate state which cannot be described or conceived. The Buddha himself resolutely refused to describe this state; he spoke of it only in negatives; it was "not born, not made, not compounded, not become." What he taught was the way to reach this state; this was man's highest knowledge.

We find a similar way of approaching the ultimate truth in the Upanishads. They are not philosophical treatises or speculations about the nature of God or the universe like the writings of the contemporary Greek philosophers. They are the record of an experience and they are intended to lead to the same experience. The Indian mind has never been content to know "about" God, it has always sought to know God, to "realize" him, to experience his presence not in the imagination or in the intellect but in the "ground" of the soul, the substance of the soul, from which all the faculties spring. This is the inner meaning of the Upanishads. The seers look out on this world and seek to penetrate beyond the senses and beyond rational thought to the hidden mystery, which lies "behind" and "within" everything. "What," they ask, "is that on which all this is woven? What is that which moves all this from within?"[6] Then they look on the human body and seek to discover the "self" which lies behind it. There is the famous story of Svetaketu in the Chandogya Upanishad, whose father tells him to take the seed of a tree and to break it to find the hidden essence of the tree. The father asks him: "What do you see?" "Nothing," he replies. Then the father says: "My son, that subtle essence which you do not see, truly from that subtle essence this great tree exists." Here we can see the precise process by which the Indian mind passes beyond the visible form and grasps the hidden essence by which things exist. And then the Upanishad rises to the supreme intuition of Indian thought: "That which is the subtle essence this whole world has for its self, That is the real, that is the Self, and Thou, Svetaketu, art That."[7]

This is the record of the decisive moment in Indian history, the discovery of the identity of the *Brahman* and the *Atman*. Behind all the appearances of the visible world is the one reality of the *Brahman*, and behind all the appearances of the body with its imagination and its thought is the reality of the *Atman,* the Self. This underlying reality is known not by reasoning but by direct experience. The Self is experienced in its own "ground," in the substance of its being, and knows itself in its identity with the "ground" or substance of the universe. This experience underlies all the teaching of the Upanishads and all subsequent Hindu thought. It was the experience of Ramana Maharshi, to name but one, in the present century, as it was the experience of Sankara in the eighth and of the seers of the Upanishads in the sixth century before Christ. But the difficulty in regard to this experience is that, since it transcends both speech and thought, it can never be properly conceived or expressed. It can only be indicated or be pointed out by means of metaphors and symbols and analogical terms.

This is what we find in the Upanishads. They are not rational discourses in the manner of Plato's Dialogues, not systems of philosophy like those of Aristotle or Aquinas. They are mystical and symbolical discourses, written some in verse and some in prose, communicating a direct intuition, and they are intended to awaken the same intuition in the mind of the reader and to lead to the same kind of experience. This is why in the past it was customary for the disciple to be initiated into this teaching by a *Guru,* that is a teacher who had himself had experience of the mystery and was able to communicate it to others. The Upanishads are the discourses of such "gurus" or "rishis," that is inspired men, who use the language of poetry and symbolism to communicate their thought. We can see a good example of this in what is probably the earliest of all the Upanishads, the Brihadaranyaka, where it is said: "What is the appearance of this Person? It is like a saffron colored garment, like white wool, like cochineal, like the flame of fire, like the white lotus, like sudden lightning. He who knows this attains glory like sudden lightning." Here we have a series of images intended to awaken the sense of the mysterious splendor of the divine Being. But since every image is utterly inadequate before the hidden mystery of the ultimate truth, the Upanishad goes on: "Now therefore this is the teaching, not this, not this—*neti, neti*—for there is nothing higher than this, that he is 'not this.'"[8]

We can see in this the precise path by which the Upanishads approach the divine mystery, which is also the ultimate truth. They first proceed by the way of affirmation, using images and symbols to represent the mystery, then they follow the way of negation, denying everything that has been affirmed, because ultimately we can only say of the divine mystery, that it is "not this, not this." This shows the extreme difficulty about all language concerning God, or rather the Godhead. For we can make meaningful, though still analogical, statements about God in his relation to man or the universe, as Creator or

Lord or Savior, but of the ultimate mystery of the Godhead we can only speak in negative terms. It is the inexpressible mystery before which all speech and thought fall away. Perhaps the nearest we can come to expressing the inexpressible is in the words of the Mandukya Upanishad: "It is unseen, incapable of being spoken of, ungraspable, without any distinctive marks, unthinkable, unnameable, the essence of the knowledge of the Self, that into which the world is resolved, the peaceful, the benign, the non-dual." Then the Upanishad adds: "This is the Self, this is to be known."[9]

Thus we are faced with the paradox that the ultimate truth, that which alone gives meaning to life, cannot be expressed, cannot in any ordinary sense be known. And yet it is above all to be known. "When this is known," as it is said elsewhere, "all is known." But it is not known by sense or reason; it is known by an intuitive wisdom, which transcends our ordinary consciousness as much as rational knowledge transcends the knowledge of the senses. Yet if negation is the primary way of expressing this mystery, there is yet one affirmation which has always been considered to point to it more clearly than any other. This is the term *saccidananda*. This term does not properly express or describe the mystery, but it signifies it more perfectly than any other words can do. The ultimate reality, the ultimate truth, is "sat"—being, "cit"—consciousness, and "ananda"—bliss. This is as near as we can come to an affirmation of the nature of the Godhead. That the divine mystery is Being is clearly affirmed by the Katha Upanishad, where it is said: "Not by speech, not by mind, not by sight can he be apprehended. How can he be apprehended except by one who says, He is."[10] But this "being," which is affirmed of the Godhead, is not being in the ordinary sense, it is not the being of the logician or the philosopher. It is the transcendent mystery of being, beyond speech and thought. Coleridge has expressed this idea of the mystery of being in a remarkable passage where he says: "Hast thou ever raised thy mind to the consideration of existence in and by itself, as the mere act of existing? Hast thou ever said to thyself thoughtfully, It is!, heedless at that moment whether it were a man before you or a flower or a grain of sand, without reference in short to this or that particular mode or form of existence? If thou hast indeed attained to this, then thou wilt have felt the presence of a mystery which must have fixed thy spirit in awe and wonder.... If thou hast mastered this intuition of absolute existence, then thou wilt have learned likewise that it was this and no other which in early ages seized the nobler minds, the elect among men, with a sort of sacred horror. This it was which first caused them to feel in themselves something infinitely greater than our individual nature." It is this intuition of being, of the fundamental mystery of existence, which underlies all Hindu thought and finds expression in the Upanishads and the whole tradition of the Vedanta.

But this mystery of being is apprehended not merely as a concept as in Greek thought but as an experience. Being is experienced in consciousness of Being, not as the object but as the subject of thought. The being which is known is the *Atman*, the Self, the Person in its ultimate depth, and it is known not by an image or a concept but in an experience of identity. "An ocean is that one seer without any duality," it is said in the Brihadaranyaka Upanishad, and "non-duality" is the most fundamental character of this experience of being. Thus it is said: "When there is duality then one sees another, smells another, hears another, speaks to another, thinks of another, knows another. But when the Self is all this, how should one smell another, see another, hear another, speak to another, think of another, know another? How should one know him by whom one knows all this? How, beloved, should one know the knower?"[11]

This then is the knowledge which the Upanishads were intended to impart, the knowledge of the Self, the knower, which is the subject not the object of thought, the ground alike of being and of thought. And this knowledge is a knowledge by identity, a consciousness of the identity of being and thought, in which all duality and multiplicity are transcended. The mind transcends all images and concepts and knows itself in the very ground of its being. But in this reflection on itself, the mind discovers the infinity of Being in which it is grounded. It knows itself in the source of its being and of all being, in the source of all matter and life and consciousness. It discovers the identity of the *Brahman* and the *Atman*, the source of being both of the universe and of the self, the ultimate truth, the ultimate reality. Such is the claim of the Upanishads and of all Hindu tradition. It is a claim which cannot be strictly verified, because this knowledge transcends all ordinary forms of consciousness and cannot therefore be properly expressed. The evidence for it is to be found in the consistency with which this experience has been proclaimed and described from the time of the Upanishads until the present day, and in the quality of life and thought which is manifest in those who claim to have had this experience. Though transcending thought and expression, it has yet been the source of the most profound philosophy, the most exalted forms of art and the deepest expressions of religious life.

This brings us to the third aspect of this mystery, that of *ananda* or bliss. This consciousness of being in non-duality is the source of endless bliss. It is beautifully compared in the Upanishads to the bliss of a man in the embrace of his wife: "As a man when embraced by a beloved wife knows nothing that is without, nothing that is within, thus this Person when embraced by the intelligent Self knows nothing that is without, nothing that is within."[12] For this knowledge is not a bare, abstract knowledge of a merely rational consciousness; it is life and peace and joy. The soul enters into that depth of being, where all the powers of its being are gathered together. It is at the source of life, of the life of matter as well as of the mind; it is also at the source of love. For in this source of Being is the satisfaction of all desire. As it is said again in the Brihadraranyaka Upanishad: "Verily, not for the sake of the husband is the husband dear, but for the sake of the Self, (the *Atman*, the Supreme Person). Verily, not for the sake of the wife is the wife dear, but for the sake of the Self,"[13] and so through all human relationships. It is this ultimate truth, this ultimate reality, which is the object of all human desire, without which no desire can ever be satisfied. We mistake the shadows of this passing world for the light which they reflect, and it is only when we discover the source of their being that our desire is satisfied.

This, then, is the mystery of Being, of Truth, the Absolute, whatever we may like to call it, which is revealed in the Upanishads and to which all subsequent Hindu tradition bears witness. This experience has received different conceptual expressions, some of which may appear to be contradictory, yet in its full scope and depth it embraces all these conceptions. It is a mystical experience, transcending all concepts and capable of receiving different conceptual formulations. It can be compared to the Buddhist experience of *Nirvana* or the Void, to the Taoist experience of the "great *Tao*" and is certainly one of the decisive experiences of humanity. What we have now to ask is, what is the relation of this experience to the religious and philosophical experience of the West, in particular to the Hebrew experience of a personal God, to the Greek discovery of the Logos and to the Christian experience of the Trinity.

It must be remembered that though the Hebrew habitually conceived God as a Person and did not hesitate to use anthropomorphic language about him, yet he always retained the sense of the divine being as a mystery. This was expressed by saying that no man could ever "see God" or that to "see God" was to die, and was reinforced by the absolute prohibition against making any image of God. The throne of Yahweh in the temple at Jerusalem was an empty seat—the "mercy-seat"—and it is said that when the Roman general Pompey entered the "holy of holies" in the temple of Jerusalem to see what was there he found nothing. Thus the Hebrew was habituated to thinking of God as having no likeness on earth. In the beginning, no doubt, Yahweh was a God of thunder and lightning, who dwelt in the storm clouds of Mount Sinai, but in the course of time this concept was refined so that he came to be conceived as a Being of transcendent mystery, whom no man could approach, and the storm clouds became the cloud of glory which surrounded him and hid him from mortal eyes. Moreover, Yahweh was essentially a "holy" God. Now holiness originally signified "separation"—to be holy was to be "set apart," whether it was a man or a thing—and Yahweh was holy because he was "set apart," transcendent, "wholly other." In the

Prophets this conception of holiness was reinforced by that of moral holiness—Yahweh was the God of absolute moral perfection, absolute justice, before which man trembled and which convicted him of sin. It is this sense of absolute moral perfection, of absolute justice and yet of infinite mercy, which distinguishes the Hebrew conception of God. It was this that led him to bow down before the transcendent mystery of the Godhead, manifested both in nature and in the trials and sufferings of human life, as we see it depicted in the book of Job.

In the New Testament, though God is spoken of as a Father in the closest intimacy with man, yet the sense of mystery is never absent. St. John says: "No man has ever seen God,"[14] and St. Paul speaks of him as "dwelling in inaccessible light."[15] Yet in the New Testament no less than in the Old, God is always conceived in relation to man. There is no speculation about the divine nature in itself. It is true that the later epistles of St. Paul speak of God as "eternal, immortal, invisible,"[16] and this concept is implied in all the thought of the New Testament, but we have to wait for the Greek Fathers before we see this concept of the divine nature developed. For the Greek Fathers it is an axiom that God is beyond all description and cannot properly be named. Thus Clement of Alexandria says: "The deity is without form and nameless. Though we ascribe names, they are not to be taken in their strict meaning; when we call him one, good, mind, existence, Father, God, Creator,

Lord, we are not conferring a name on him. Being unable to do more, we use these appellations of honor in order that our thought may have something to rest on."[17] Again, Origen says: "The true nature of God cannot be comprehended by our thought. If there is anything we are able to conceive or understand about God, we are bound to believe him far superior to anything we can conceive."[18]

But it was in the Syrian monk, who wrote under the name of Dionysius the Areopagite in the sixth century, that we find the whole problem of the nature of God and of our human understanding of it systematically worked out for the first time. This writer had absorbed the doctrine of Neo-Platonism, which, with its conception of the One that transcends all speech and thought and can only be known in an ecstasy when the mind passes beyond itself, is the doctrine which comes nearest in the West to the doctrine of the Vedanta, and indeed it may be that at this point there was actually a direct influence of Indian thought on the European mind. However this may be, we find in him a Christian idea of God, which comes very close to that of the Vedanta. Dionysius begins from the conception of what he calls the "superessential Godhead." By this he means that the Godhead is above all being no less than it is above all thought. Thus he says: "As for the super-essence of the supreme Godhead (if we would define the transcendence of its transcendent Goodness), it is not lawful to any lover of that Truth, which is above all truth, to celebrate It as Reason or Power or Mind, or Life or Being, but rather as utterly surpassing all condition, movement, life, imagination, conjecture, name, discourse, thought, conception, being, rest, dwelling, union, limit, infinity, everything that exists."[19] Thus, just as in the Vedanta, we have to pass beyond every thought and everything that exists—*neti, neti*—in order to reach the supreme Godhead. But since the Godhead is the cause of everything that exists, it can be known in a certain sense from existing things. All energy, all life and all thought come from this source and are therefore in one sense contained in it. Thus Dionysius is led to frame the three ways of knowledge of God, the way of affirmation, the way of negation and the way of transcendence. We first affirm that God is Being, Truth, Goodness, Light, Life, Wisdom, since he is the source of all these things; so we call him Creator, Father, Lord. But then immediately we have to deny what we have affirmed, since the Godhead infinitely transcends all being, truth, goodness, as we conceive them. So we are led to the way of transcendence. All things exist in God, since he is their cause, yet they exist in him in a way that totally transcends their present mode of existence. Thus Dionysius writes: "The Universal and Transcendent Cause must be both nameless and also possess the names of all things, in order that it may be a universal dominion, the Center of creation, on which all things depend as their cause and origin and goal... originating and maintaining and perfecting all things... and all this in one single, ceaseless and transcendent act... for it contains all things beforehand in itself after a simple and uncircumscribed manner."[20]

Thus we arrive at a perfect conception of the nature of the Godhead as far as it can be conceived. In itself it is beyond all name and form; all being, conception or expression. Yet since it is the source of everything that exists, all matter, life, consciousness, reason and will, these things must somehow exist in it, but in a way which transcends all conception. So Dionysius concludes that if we would attain to the knowledge of the supreme Godhead, we can only do so by a kind of "unknowing"; we have to pass beyond images and concepts into the darkness of an "unknowing" which exceeds all knowing. So, he says: "We press on upwards according to our powers to behold in simple unity the Truth perceived by spiritual contemplation, and leaving behind all human notion of god-like things we still the activity of our minds and reach into the Superessential Light, wherein all kinds of knowledge have their limits in a transcendent, inexpressible manner, so that we cannot conceive or utter it... seeing that it surpasses all things and wholly exceeds our knowledge."[21] Thus we can see how Christian thought arrives like Hindu thought at the idea of the divine being as a hidden mystery, transcending thought, which can only be known by a power beyond reason, which gives a knowledge transcending all knowledge in an actual experience of the divine.

At the same time, Christian tradition like Hindu tradition recognizes that though the divine nature cannot be properly known or expressed, yet there are certain terms which are particularly appropriate to indicate its nature by analogy. The first of these is Being. The name of God, which was revealed to Moses in the Old Testament, was Yahweh, which is derived from the root of the verb "to be." The exact meaning of it is disputed by scholars. Some would translate it as "I will be," signifying God's continued active presence among his people; others take it to mean "I cause to be" signifying the creative power of God. But the traditional translation is "I am," God is "He who is," which takes us back to the affirmation of the Katha Upanishad, "He is." The Greek Fathers and after them the Latin Fathers and Doctors from the beginning understood this text of Exodus as an affirmation of the nature of God as Being itself. Thus St. Gregory of Nyssa says: "Nothing exists with a real existence except the Supreme Being, the first and sovereign cause of all beings."[22] St. Thomas Aquinas says that "being" is the most proper name of God, because it is the least determined of all terms. Every other name adds some kind of form or determination to being, but being itself is not determined in any way. There is no necessary limit to the act of existence and in this way we can conceive of God as the pure act of existence, as existence itself, absolutely free and undertermined. In this sense, God is Being itself, not a particular being but the universal ground of all being; not determined by space and time and therefore infinite and eternal; absolutely simple, absolutely full, absolutely unchanging, because it lacks nothing and has nothing to acquire. St. John Damascene, the doctor of Greek orthodoxy, declares that God is "an infinite ocean of being." Thus Christian tradition joins Hindu tradition in seeing God as an "ocean of being without duality," for to say that the divine being is pure existence without any limitation or qualification is to say that it is absolutely simple and "without duality."

But to say that God is Being itself is to say that he is also consciousness, for to lack consciousness is to be deficient in being; it is an imperfect mode of existence. It is an axiom of Greek thought that being and knowing are correlative. The more fully and completely a thing exists the more perfectly conscious it is. The lower forms of life are enclosed in their own existence, unable to know themselves or to know others. When nature reaches consciousness in man, then nature begins to know itself, to reflect upon itself and so to organize its own existence. Consciousness is the reflection of being on itself, but in man this reflection is always imperfect. We come to know ourselves only through the knowledge of external things. By reflection on ourselves, on our thought and our action, we come to know ourselves, but never normally attain to a perfect intuition of ourselves. Yet it is to this intuition of ourselves that we constantly aspire. It is at this point that Hindu thought seems to mark the greatest insight of the human spirit. For the Hindu sage has always claimed to have reached this intuition of the Self. The experience of the *Atman* in Hindu tradition is the soul's direct intuition of itself, in which subject and object are no longer distinguished; the knower, the thing known and the act of knowing are all one. In this experience the soul goes beyond itself, that is beyond its phenomenal being, and reaches the transcendent Self in the consciousness of infinite, transcendent Being.

In Christian tradition this aspect of the divine nature as transcendent consciousness is known as the Logos. The Logos is one of the most fundamental concepts of Greek philosophy, which was first formulated by Heraclitus in the sixth century before Christ, to describe the rational order in the universe. The Logos is the immanent principle of unity and order in the universe and at the same time the principle of reason in man. Reason in man is a reflection, a particular manifestation of the universal reason that governs the world. This concept of the Logos became the basis of the whole philosophical tradition among the Stoics, but it also entered Christian tradition, when St. John in his Gospel described Christ as the Logos. This is the precise point of the meeting of Greek philosophy and Hebrew revelation which was to determine the whole development of Christian theology. In St. John's view the Logos is not merely the immanent principle of order in the universe; it is a transcendent principle—the Logos was "with God" and the Logos "was God"[23]—but at the same time it is the source both of life and reason in man—"in Him was life and the life was the light of men,"[24] and it is the source of all creation—"all things were made by Him and without Him was not anything made that was made."[25]

This concept of the Logos was to provide the Christian faith with a philosophical basis which was all-embracing. The Logos was the principle of all creation, of everything that exists; it was the principle of reason and intelligence, that is of consciousness, in man; and finally it was the principle of wisdom and self-consciousness in God. In the Old Testament God is described as possessing a Wisdom by which he created the universe; this Wisdom is called "an effulgence from the everlasting light and an unspotted mirror of the action of God and an image of his Goodness."[26] "Being one," it is said, "she has power to do all things and remaining in herself renews all things."[27] "She reaches from end to end of the world with full strength and orders all things graciously."[28] In the New Testament this conception of the Wisdom of God is identified with the Word of God who is described as "the effulgence of the glory of God and the very image of his being."[29] Thus we arrive at the idea of the Logos as a "reflection" of God, a mirror in which the divine being beholds itself. In other words in the Logos or Word, the Supreme Being knows itself in an act of reflection on itself. While in the human mind, as we have said, this reflection of the mind on itself is normally imperfect, in God we conceive of a perfect reflection of Being on itself. God knows himself in a perfect image or likeness of himself, which is the very expression of his Being. In us the word expresses something of ourselves—the great poet mirrors himself in his poetry—but in God the Word expresses the whole being of God; the Word is a full and perfect expression of God. This is the full and perfect intimacy of self-knowledge for which we crave.

We can see from this how closely the Christian concept of the Logos corresponds with the Hindu concept of the *Atman,* the Self. The Logos is the divine Self-consciousness, the Self of God. In it God knows himself, reflects himself, is present to himself. All these are, of course, analogies, by which we try to represent the divine nature in terms of our human knowledge and experience. Yet this is not merely a game, which we play with words, since it is based on the actual experience of the seers. It is the claim of the Hindu seers that they have had an actual experience of the divine consciousness; this is the very essence of the experience of *Saccidananda.* In the same way according to Christian tradition the saint through his "participation in the divine nature"[30] comes to share in the divine wisdom and knowledge. This is realized, above all, of course, according to Christian faith, in Jesus Christ himself. He was conscious of himself as sharing the being, life and consciousness of God. This he expressed by speaking of himself as the "Son" of the Father, and declaring that the Son "knows" the Father as the Father "knows" the Son. These are, of course, anthropomorphic terms, but they signify on the one hand that the Logos comes forth from the Father, who is the Source of Being, and exists in a relation of total dependence on him; and on the other that the Word is the conscious reflection of the divine being and exists in conscious relation to it. For knowledge is essentially relationship. To know someone or something is to enter into relation with them: that person or that thing becomes present to me and in a sense becomes part of me and yet remains distinct. If there is no distinction there is no knowledge. Thus we have to conceive in the divine nature a kind of relation analogous to the relation which we find in the human experience of knowledge. The Father beholds himself in the Son, reflects himself in the Son, is present to himself in the Son, as the Son in the Father. Yet there is no "duality" in the proper sense. There is an absolute identity of nature between the Father and the Son; the Son is the radiance of the Godhead, the Light of Truth reflecting its source.

We are here, of course, in the realm of mystery, in which all human terms are inadequate; we are touching on the ultimate depth of all human experience. On this matter of the divine consciousness, there are differences within Hinduism itself, between Sankara, Ramanuja and Madhva. All that we can do is to place the Christian experience of the divine consciousness beside that of the great doctors of the Vedanta and compare them with one another. Sankara conceives the *Brahman* as pure consciousness of being without any distinction whatever. It is the very essence of his philosophy that the *Brahman*, the ultimate reality, is pure consciousness without any "marks" or distinctions, "without qualities" *(Nirguna)*. Ramanuja on the contrary, holds that Isvara, the Lord, who is also the "highest *Brahman*" is a personal, self-conscious being. He knows himself as the possessor of "innumerable auspicious attributes;" he is *Saguna*, the plenitude of personal being, possessing attributes which are really distinct from his essence. This gives us a personal god, which may satisfy the heart, but he loses the absolute simplicity of the *Brahman* of Sankara and can hardly satisfy the philosopher. Madhva seems to come nearer the truth, when he declares that the *Brahman* is the supreme person, who has innumerable attributes of perfection which are, however, identical with his essence, and therefore do not modify the simplicity of his nature.

The Christian God is the absolutely simple Being of Sankara who is also pure consciousness and bliss, but he is also a personal God. What this signifies is that in the depths of the divine being, in the ultimate ground of the Godhead, there is a plenitude of personal being, that is of knowledge and love.

Though the Godhead infinitely transcends all limitations of personality, as we know them in this world, yet it also includes all the values of personality in a transcendent way. If by "person" we mean some kind of limitation of being, then clearly God is not a person at all, since he is the absolute plenitude of being without any limitation. But if by a person we mean conscious being, a being capable of knowledge and love, then surely God is personal in the fullest sense, since he is the plenitude of conscious being, in which is found the plenitude of blissful love.

This brings us to the last aspect of the Godhead, that of bliss, *ananda*. As there is in human nature a capacity for knowledge, of receiving the forms of things into itself, so that the world becomes present to us and we become present to ourselves, so there is a corresponding capacity of love, or self-communication, by which we seek to give ourselves to others and find our happiness in this. So in God we have to conceive by analogy that as he is infinite Being in perfect consciousness of itself, so there is in him a delight in being, a pure joy of being, by which in knowing himself he rejoices in himself. This is the meaning of *ananda*, the pure joy of conscious existence. But there is more than this. If there is in God the capacity of self-knowledge, there is also the capacity of self-communication. It was one of the great achievements of the Vedanta that it was able to receive into itself the current of *bhakti*, or devotion to a personal God, and so to conceive of God as love. We find this first of all in the Bhagavad Gita, but it has a long history of development among the Vaishnavite and Saivite dev-otees, with their wonderful conception of divine grace, by which God gives himself to his devotee. Yet there perhaps has always been a certain conflict in Hindu tradition between the concept of a personal God who manifests himself in love and the advaitic conception of the *Brahman* as the pure bliss of conscious exis-tence without relationship to another.

In Christian tradition this aspect of the Godhead as bliss is represented by the Holy Spirit. As there is in God a Word, by which he knows himself and all things, so there is in him a Spirit, by which he communicates himself. As the Word corresponds to the intellect in man, so the Spirit corresponds to the will. There is in God a pure will of love, a pure act of self-giving by which he ceaselessly communicates himself. As the Father knows himself in the Son, and the Son in the Father, so Father and Son com-municate in the love of the Holy Spirit. The Holy Spirit is this expression of love within the Godhead, the relation of love which unites the persons of the Godhead, and yet there is in it no "duality," but an identity of nature and consciousness in the bliss of love. Thus the bliss of the Godhead in the Christian view is the overflowing love of God, the mysterious communication of love within the Godhead. Again we must remind ourselves that we are speaking in terms of analogy. We are trying to conceive the nature of God in terms of our human experience of being, knowledge and love. We apprehend that God is the Source of all being, knowledge and love. The being, knowledge and love which we experience in our human lives are a reflection in us of the being, knowledge and love of God. As we grow in knowledge and love by our daily experience, we begin to experience more consciously this presence of God as the source of knowledge and love in our lives and so grow towards the experience of the divine being, knowledge and bliss. In the great masters of the spiritual life, in the Buddha, in the Krishna of the Gita, in Ramakrishna and Ramana Maharshi, we recognize human beings who have experienced something of the inner depth of the divine life and who have communicated to others something of this mystery. In Jesus Christ according to Christian faith we find a human being who experienced this mystery of the divine consciousness in a unique way. He knew himself in relation to God as Son of the Father, that is he knew himself to be one with God and yet distinct from him, in an identity of nature but distinction of person. At the same time he experienced the divine love as a gift of the Spirit, a self-communication by which the Father eternally gave himself to him and which he in turn was able to communicate to his disciples. It is from this experience of the mystery of knowledge and love in the Godhead that the Christian doctrine of the Trinity was evolved.

Thus Christian faith discovers within the abyss of the Godhead, that divine darkness of which

Dionysius speaks, a mystery of personal communion, in which all that we can conceive of wisdom and knowledge, of love and bliss, is contained and yet which infinitely transcends our conception. The terms we use of being, knowledge, love, nature, person, relation are all terms of analogy. The Godhead remains that unfathomable abyss, which transcends all human thought, of which Hindu, Buddhist and Christian mystics alike speak, and yet in that abyss are contained, though in a transcendent way, all that we can conceive of being, truth, goodness, beauty, grace, love, wisdom and immortality. This is the mystery which continues to haunt us, ever drawing us towards itself and challenging us to go beyond all human concepts and experience and to ascend above the whole creation into the depths of the divine darkness. Let the great Dionysius have the last word: "I counsel you, that in the earnest exercise of mystical contemplation you leave the senses and the activity of the intellect, and all that the senses and the intellect can perceive, and all things in this world of nothingness and that world of being, and that your understanding being laid to rest, you strive towards a union with him whom neither being nor understanding can contain. For by the unceasing and absolute renunciation of yourself and all things you shall in purity cast all things aside and be released from all, and so shall you be led upwards to the Ray of that divine darkness, which exceeds all existence."[31]

II. CREATION AND INCARNATION

Purnam adah, purnam idam, purnat purnam udacyate
Purnasya purnam adaya purnam evavasisyate.

That is full; this is full. The full comes out of the full.
Taking the full from the full, the full itself remains.[32]

THIS VERSE, WHICH FORMS the invocation of the Isa Upanishad expresses in a marvellous way the mystery of creation. The world comes forth from God and exists in the fullness of being, and yet the world takes nothing from God and adds nothing to him. God remains ever the same. This is the mystery of creation, and it is well to emphasize that it is and remains mystery like God himself. It is only when we recognize that we are dealing with a mystery which transcends the understanding that we can begin to make sense of creation. All merely rational explanations of the universe are inadequate; at best they can point towards a reality which they cannot explain.

In the history of the Vedanta there have been different answers to this question of the nature of the universe and its relation to the ultimate reality. This seems to me to be one of the most interesting problems raised by the Vedanta and the point at which a comparison with Christian doctrine can be most revealing. To my mind the Vedanta has never found a completely satisfying answer to this problem, and this may well be the point at which Christian faith could add something to the understanding of the Vedanta and at the same time at which Christian faith could also learn to express itself more adequately in terms of the Vedanta.

The theory of the universe which is most commonly accepted by Hindus today is the *advaita* doctrine of Sankara, but it must always be remembered that the doctrine of Sankara has met in the past with a strong and even violent opposition from other doctors of the Vedanta and has more recently been subjected to a severe criticism by Sri Aurobindo. It remains one of the most fascinating theories of human genius and one which does not cease to attract even when one may disagree. This doctrine is by no means so simple as it is often made out to be. Sankara was deeply aware of the mysterious character of the *Brahman*, the ultimate reality. He never fell into the facile rationalism, which some of his followers have shown. He was strongly opposed to the Buddhist doctrine of the Void (*sunya*), which was prevalent at his time and which to many might seem almost identical with his own. Indeed, it was largely through his determined opposition that Buddhism seems to have been driven out of India. According to the Buddhist doctrine, which was propounded by Nagarjuna, the universe is without any ultimate reality or consistency; it is fundamentally "empty" or void. The appearance of a world with things which originate and cease to exist is a pure illusion of the mind. Reality is "like the sky"—without origination or cessation; the truth is "stainless, changeless and quiescent."

Against this doctrine Sankara affirmed that though the external world has no absolute reality, yet it has a certain reality. He described it in an admirable phrase as "an appearance of being, without origin, inexpressible in terms of being as of not being." In other words, Sankara recognized the mysterious character of the world; it is neither being nor not-being, neither completely real nor completely unreal, and its origin cannot be explained. Thus there is a certain realism in Sankara's doctrine; against the Buddhist he always insisted the world is real to our senses, and our reason must allow it a certain reality. Yet he affirmed on the other hand, that in the highest mode of knowledge above sense and reason—in *paravidya* as opposed to *aparavidya*—the world is seen to have no distinct reality at all. The world in its ultimate reality is identical with the *Brahman*, with absolute reality. All differences which appear to exist are apparent, not real. They are "superimposed" on the one absolutely simple reality of the *Brahman*.

Thus in Sankara's view the ultimate reality is "without duality"—it is an absolute, simple identity of being—and in the highest state of consciousness, that of *paravidya*, the human being is conscious of this identity of being. He realizes the absolute, unchanging state of being in pure consciousness, and realizes at the same time that all the apparent multiplicity of this world with its "name and form" is a "superimposition" on this pure identity of being. The world has the reality of an appearance of being to our present mode of consciousness but when we awake to a higher consciousness, we discover that it is a mere appearance like a dream or the illusion created by a juggler, or according to his favorite simile, like the form of a snake which is "superimposed" on that of a rope. When we see the world as it really is we see it as *Brahman*, as the absolute being, and know ourselves in identity with this being. We then realize the meaning of the "great sayings" of the Upanishads: "I am *Brahman*," "Thou are That."

There can be no doubt about the grandeur of Sankara's system or the depth of its insight. He was one of the great philosophers of all time. He was at once a mystic with a penetrating insight into the nature of ultimate truth and a logician who could create a coherent system of rational thought based on this insight. There can be no doubt also that Sankara's doctrine has a firm basis in the Upanishads. It conforms to the deepest intuitions of the Upanishads—to the *mahavakyas*—round which he built his philosophy. There is a beautiful consistency in his doctrine, which continues to fascinate the mind; in a sense it answers all questions and resolves all problems. But this achievement is won at a cost which it is difficult to pay. It demands that we admit the ultimate unreality of all distinct forms of being, not only of the external world, but of the human consciousness and of a personal God. From the earliest times, as we have said, there has been resistance to Sankara's doctrine within the Vedanta itself. Though it answers to certain aspects of the Upanishads—perhaps to the most important—yet it seems to leave others out of account. The Upanishads affirm the non-duality of the ultimate truth, but they seem also to allow a place to a real multiplicity of being and to a personal God.

The opposition to Sankara was crystallized by Ramanuja in the eleventh century and later by Madhva in the thirteenth. Both of them were deeply influenced by the current of *bhakti*, or devotion to a personal God, which grew up in the Bhagavad Gita in the first or second century before Christ, and was developed by the great Tamil poets, the Alvars and the Nayanmars in the seventh and eighth centuries. It was this devotion to a personal God, who, while retaining the absolute character of Being, Knowledge and Bliss, which derived from the Upanishads, was also worshipped as the supreme Lord (whether as the Krishna of the Gita, or as Siva—the Gracious one — who appears in the Svetasvatara Upanishad) which caused a reaction to the teaching of Sankara. For Sankara the supreme Being was *nirguna Brahman*, that is *Brahman* "without qualities or attributes," but for Ramanuja and Madhva *Brahman* was *saguna*, that is "with qualities." He was the supreme Lord possessed of innumerable auspicious attributes. We must beware, however, of saying that for Sankara the *Brahman* is the impersonal absolute, while for Ramanuja and Madhva he is the personal God. The *Brahman* of Sankara is absolute, being in the plenitude of conscious bliss, and such a being cannot properly be called impersonal, since consciousness is of the very essence of personality. We may call him rather "suprapersonal" in so far as he transcends all conceivable limitations of personal being.

Yet it remains true that for Sankara the *Brahman* is without relationship of any sort, and therefore, it must be supposed, without love. But for Ramanuja God is above all a God of love. He is a personal being, free from all imperfections, possessed of all auspicious attributes. He is the Lord (Isvara), omnipotent and omniscient, possessing the fullness of Being, knowledge and bliss, but also of grace and love. "We know from scripture that there is a supreme person, whose nature is absolute bliss and goodness: who is fundamentally antagonistic to all evil: who is the cause of the origination, sustentation and dissolution of the world: who differs in nature from all other beings: who is all-knowing: who by his mere thought and will accomplishes all his purposes: who is an ocean of kindness as it were, for all who depend on him: who is all-merciful: who is immensurably raised above all possibility of one being equal or superior to him: whose name is the highest *Brahman*."[33] Thus Ramanuja establishes the personal God as the supreme Being, attributing to him all the perfections of the *Brahman*.

At the same time Ramanuja admits the distinct reality of nature and of souls, the world of unconscious and conscious beings. The multiplicity of the world is not unreal for him; it is no less real than the *Brahman*. It is, in fact, part of the *Brahman*. This is what leads Ramanuja to his doctrine of *Visishtadvaita*, or "qualified" *advaita*. The *Brahman* is "non-dual," that is to say it is absolutely simple in itself; but it is "qualified" by nature and by souls. Nature and souls are evolved from the *Brahman*. They remain latent in the *Brahman* from the beginning, and then when creation is determined, they come forth from the *Brahman*. The *Brahman* says: "May I become manifold," and the world comes into being. They are evolved from the very substance of the *Brahman*, which is the material as well as the efficient cause of the world. According to the simile used in the Upanishads, as the spider comes out with its thread, so the world comes forth from the *Brahman*.

What then is the relation between the world and the *Brahman*? Ramanuja replies that it is the relation between a substance and its attributes; just as a lotus may be white or blue or red, and thus has different attributes, yet remains essentially a lotus, so, he says, the *Brahman* while remaining essentially the same possesses an infinite multiplicity of qualities or attributes, which constitute this world of multiplicity. The *Brahman* is the substance of which "this all" is a quality; the *Brahman* is the subject, of which all other beings are predicates. In other words, the world is constructed in terms of subject and predicate, but the *Brahman* is the one ultimate subject, of which everything else is a predicate. But this does not mean that the world had no substantiality of its own. Ramanuja explains this by the analogy of soul and body. The soul is a substance which is "qualified" by the body, yet the body is in turn a substance with its own qualities. So also, Ramanuja contends that the *Brahman* is the soul of which the universe constitutes the body. "The world," he says, "of sentient and non-sentient beings is the body of the Supreme Person, who rules it from within." He defines a body as "any substance which a sentient soul is capable of completely controlling and supporting for its own purpose and which stands to the soul in an entirely subordinate relation."[34] In this sense, then, he says that the world is the Body of God and God is the Soul of the world.

Yet Ramanuja contends that though the world may be called a "part" (*amsa*) or mode (*prakara*) of the divine being, yet God is in no way affected by the imperfection of the world. "The *Brahman*," he says, "is essentially opposed to all evil, of uniform goodness, differing in nature from all beings other than itself, in eternal possession of all its wishes, supremely blessed, yet has for its body the entire universe with all its sentient and non-sentient beings, and constitutes the Self of the universe."[35] How this may be he explains in this way. The *Brahman* exists in itself in the plenitude of being, knowledge and bliss, unaffected by anything external to itself. Nature (*prakriti*) and souls exist eternally as "modes" of the divine being, knowledge and bliss, not of themselves but in total dependence on the *Brahman*, as modes of his being. Souls exist in this state necessarily as modes of the divine being, having no connection with any body. Nature, on the other hand, exists eternally in the *Brahman* as a mode of his being, but in an unevolved state. While souls are pure spirit existing in conscious bliss, nature is essentially unconscious and subject to change. It is to nature (*Prakrit*) that is due the evolution of the world; the world evolves from nature in continuing cycles owing to the intrinsic character of nature as a being subject to change.

Thus nature evolves from the *Brahman* as a mode of his being without in any way effecting a change in the essential nature of the *Brahman*. This evolution, though determined by principles inherent in nature herself, is yet willed by the *Brahman*, and in this sense, and in this sense alone, God can be said to "create" the world. As for souls, they are naturally as has been said, pure spirits inhering in the *Brahman* and finding their happiness in him. The soul's connection with the body comes when the soul turns away from the *Brahman* towards nature and allows herself to be captivated by it. This is the effect of *Karma*, a mysterious force which turns the soul away from God and subjects it to matter. In this sense the soul's entrance into this world is for Ramanuja an effect of sin. In his view God permits the soul to turn away from him and punishes it by making it subject to a mortal body, but at the same time this punishment is also a means for its release. For when the soul realizes its misery through its attachment to the body, it is led to turn away from the body and nature back to God, who then draws it by his grace back to himself. Thus creation for Ramanuja is an evolution of nature and souls, which takes place as a result of principles inherent in nature and souls and is not directly an effect of the divine will, nor does it in any way affect the divine being in its unchangeable goodness.

In this world, which comes into being at least indirectly by his will, the *Brahman* remains as the eternal substance, of which the changing phenomena of this world are only modes of his being. But at the same time he dwells in all things as the Lord, the

Self, the inner Ruler, who directs everything by his will and controls its evolution. So also the *Brahman* remains the Lord, the inner self of every soul, permitting it to turn from him but drawing it back to himself by his grace. The soul remains, according to Ramanuja, free to choose right or wrong, yet the Lord directs it by his inner guidance within. No action is possible without the permission of the Self, but when a soul is bent on evil, he punishes it by allowing it to follow its evil course, while, when the soul is resolved to do good, the Lord engenders in it a tendency towards the good and enables it to attain it.[36] Thus there is in Ramanuja's philosophy a profound conception of grace and free will and of the mystery of salvation. The soul has fallen under the dominion of matter and the body and become a slave to its passions, but the Lord (Isvara) desiring its salvation bestows grace upon it and enables it to turn to him. When the soul turns to him, then he draws it by his grace and awakes a deep love in it for him. It is by recognizing that its salvation depends entirely upon him, and by surrendering to him in total self-surrender (*prapatti*), that the soul eventually attains to eternal happiness and recovers the state of bliss which it had lost.

As with the doctrine of Sankara, so with that of Ramanuja, it is impossible not to admire its grandeur and comprehensiveness. At the same time it is impossible to deny that it corresponds very closely with one aspect of the doctrine of the Upanishads. If

Sankara built his whole philosophy round the "great sayings," "I am *Brahman*," "Thou are that," Ramanuja does more justice to the other aspect of the teaching of the Upanishads which gives objective reality to the world and the individual soul and speaks of *Brahman* as the Inner Ruler, the Lord. "He who dwells in the self within the self, whom the self does not know, of whom the self is the body, who also rules the self from within, He is thyself, the Ruler within, the Immortal." Again a Christian cannot but be impressed with Ramanuja's conception of a personal God, who is Being, Knowledge and Bliss in the fullness of self-consciousness, eternal, infinite and unchanging, and who yet reveals himself as a God of grace, and love, delivering souls from sin, drawing them to himself, perfecting them by his grace, and even becoming incarnate for their salvation, for such is Ramanuja's conception of the *avatara*. All this is language with which a Christian is familiar and which is like an echo of his own faith. Indeed, it is impossible to doubt that Ramanuja was truly the recipient of divine grace, which enabled him thus to penetrate into the mystery of the Person of God, of grace and of salvation.

Yet there is something in Ramanuja's conception of God which a Christian cannot accept. Though there can be no doubt that Ramanuja believed in the absolute perfection of the divine nature and intended to safeguard it by all means in his doctrine, yet by allowing that the divine nature is "qualified," that nature and souls are "parts" of God, "modes" of the divine being that the would is the body of which God is the soul, has not Ramanuja compromised the purity and simplicity of the divine nature? If nature and souls really evolve from the divine nature and constitute its body, must not God be in some way affected by the change? Even if the divine essence remains unchanged, as Ramanuja insisted, must it not be at least "accidentally" changed? Certainly Ramanuja is not a pantheist in the way of Spinoza, but can he entirely escape the charge of pantheism? Even though in his own essence God stands infinitely above the world, yet he is "accidentally" identified with it. If the world is a mode of the divine being, then we have to say that in some sense the world is God. Thus though Ramanuja's conception of God is so attractive to a Christian at first sight, there is a sense in which the *nirguna Brahman*, the absolutely unqualified, non-dual being, of Sankara is nearer to the Christian conception of God than the "qualified" being of Ramanuja.

If we want to find a conception of God, which is fully personal and yet in which God remains eternally and absolutely distinct from the universe, we have to turn to Madhva. The *dvaita*, or dualist, system of Madhva is the only system of the Vedanta which upholds a radical distinction between God and nature. Though Madhva's system has its roots in early tradition and he defended it strenuously as an authentic interpretation of the Vedas, it goes beyond any other Indian system in its insistence on the radical difference between God and nature and souls. For Madhva[37] there is a fundamental diversity in the universe, between God and man and nature, and between man and the world, and between different beings in the world. In this respect Madhva comes nearer to the Christian view of creation than any other Indian system, and there are certain features in his doctrine which suggest that he may possibly have been directly influenced by Christianity. Yet there still remains a great difference. Though nature and souls are really distinct from God, they exist eternally alongside him. Though they depend radically upon him, yet they are not precisely created by him. God, nature and souls exist eternally, God in his own perfect independence (*svabhava*), nature and souls in dependence on him, but it is nowhere said that God causes the existence of nature and souls, and this is the crucial point.

Thus I would like to suggest that the critical question in regard to the relation of the Vedanta to Christian faith is in this matter of creation. Each system of the Vedanta, as we have seen, has its own profound conception of God and his relation to the universe, but none of them is precisely that of Christian faith. Here then, I suggest is a point which needs to be studied, if we are to reach any understanding of the exact relation between Hindu and Christian philosophy. Christianity has always taken its stand on the doctrine of creation. The first words of the Bible are: "In the beginning God created the heaven and the earth,"[38] and the earliest Christian creed begins with the words: "I believe in one God, the Father Almighty, Creator of heaven and earth." This doctrine has been developed, moreover, by the Fathers and Doctors of the Church and underlies the whole system of St. Bonaventure and St. Thomas Aquinas in the Middle Ages. Yet we must remind ourselves that creation is a "mystery," that is it can never be perfectly intelligible to human reason. Yet we can say with certainty what creation is not, that is what it excludes. It excludes on the one hand the theory of Sankara that the world has no real being distinct from that of God and is in its ultimate essence identical with the being of God; and on the other hand, the theory of Ramanuja that the world is a "part" of God, or "mode" of the divine being. On the other hand, we must also avoid a conception of creation, which suggests like that of Madhva that the world and God are two separate "beings." This is often suggested by the image of God as a Maker, who produces the universe as a potter produces a pot. This gives rise to an imaginary idea of God as a being "above" the universe, who exists as it were alongside this world and directs it from above.

We must be clear from the beginning that God is not a "being," an object, which exists like other beings as an object of our thought. No person and nothing exists in the same way as God exists; the word "existence" is only used by analogy of God and creatures.

The mode of existence of the world is a wholly relative mode; God alone exists absolutely in himself and of himself and for himself; the world exists from him and through him and for him. The Christian doctrine of creation is usually expressed by saying that God created the world "out of nothing." But this phrase can be extremely misleading. It suggests that "nothing" is somehow something out of which the world is created. Its real meaning is simply that the world is created from no pre-existing matter. This was said against the view of Plato and of Greek philosophy generally, that there was a pre-existent matter, or chaos, upon which form or order was imposed by the Demiourgos. Thus creation was conceived simply as the imposition of "form" on "matter." But in the Christian view there is no pre-existent matter of any kind. The world comes wholly from God; it derives everything that it has, even its very existence, from God. To create is to give existence—its whole existence—to something. But how can this be conceived, since we have no experience of creation in this sense in our lives?

Perhaps the best analogy we can find for the act of creation is the creation, as it is significantly called, of a work of art. A work of art, a poem or a symphony, comes from the mind of the poet; it "reflects" the mind of the poet, it represents some aspect of his being; and yet it is really distinct from him. A poem is made up of words and a word is the expression of thought; it gives form to thought. In human experience a word is formed by sound in the air and thus depends on something external to the mind, but there is also an "internal" word, an expression of thought in the mind, which is less dependent on anything external. Of course, in human experience we never discover a pure "creation," the production of an idea which depends on nothing but the mind of the thinker. Our very language and capacity of speech is something which we learn from others and which depends for its exercise on others. But it is not difficult to conceive how a word, a thought, could spring up in the divine mind, which would be simply and purely the expression of this mind and would depend on nothing else. It is thus, as we have seen, that the Christian faith conceives the Word of God, as springing from the mind of the Father, as an expression of the mind itself, a reflection of his being. On this analogy we can conceive how the divine mind, reflecting on itself, can give expression to different aspects of its being. Since the mind of God is infinite, it is capable of expression in an infinite number of finite ways. In this way every finite being would be a finite expression of some aspect of the infinite mind of God. It would be an "expression" of the mind of God, a "reflection" of his being, derived entirely from God and dependent on no external being.

The fathers of the Church, especially St. Augustine, took up Plato's theory of "ideas," by which he conceived that everything on earth has its eternal idea or archetype, of which it is a kind of reflection, and conceived that these "ideas" of all things exist eternally, not in themselves, as Plato thought, but in the mind of God. Every created thing existing in time and space has its "idea," which exists eternally in the mind of God. But these ideas are not really distinct from God. In him they exist in an identity of being, and differ not really "in re" but only in our manner of conceiving them. We can see here how the Christian theory comes near to the *advaita* doctrine of Sankara. For in this theory everything, as it exists in God, exists in absolute identity of being in him. The "ideas" of God, as St. Thomas Aquinas affirms, are not really distinct from the divine nature; this is precisely how Sankara conceives multiplicity of the world as existing in identity in the *Brahman*. But the Christian view differs from Sankara by affirming that when the world is created, then God causes these ideas, which exist eternally in him in an identity of being, to begin to exist in themselves in distinction from him. Creation is the act by which God wills the distinct existence of each person and thing and causes those ideas which exist eternally in him to exist separately in time and space.

Of course, we are speaking in terms of analogy. Just as a man conceives an idea in his mind and "embodies" that idea by an act of his will in a word, or a poem or a building, so we conceive that God conceives in his mind the ideas of all things and "embodies" them by an act of will in creation. Thus the whole being of creation comes wholly from God as an expression of his mind and will. But we must be careful not to imagine that this act takes place in time. Time itself is part of the order of creation. The act of creation in God is an eternal act identical with his eternal being, by which he wills the existence of beings other than himself and causes them to exist in space and time. Space and time are therefore the condition under which the eternal and infinite being of God is reflected. Thus creation does not cause any change in God; it does not add anything to the being of God or take anything away. One may suggest as an analogy that it is as though a mirror were held up to God in which the divine being was reflected: The world has not the same kind of being as God—it has a reflected being, a wholly relative and dependent being. In this sense we can agree with Sankara that the world is neither being nor not-being.

Thus we can say that the world is a kind of reflection in space and time of the eternal and infinite being of God. But we must beware of thinking of eternity and infinity as an infinite extension in space and time. There is no extension of any kind in the being of God. The whole order of space and time is present to the mind of God in a single instant and at a single point. There is no succession of any sort to his mind, but a total and simultaneous presence. We can find an analogy for this in the way that a drama or a symphony can be present to the mind of the composer in its totality and in all its parts at a single instant; even in our own experience the more intimately we know a poem or a piece of music the more we grasp the whole and all its parts in a single comprehensive vision. It is only the imperfection of our minds, which compels us to see everything successively and at a distance. The more perfectly we comprehend anything, the more it becomes present to us in a single intuition. We can see this in the mind of a mathematician, who can see all the implications of an equation in an instant, or a psychologist, who can understand the whole complex of a character or a situation at a glance. So we can conceive that the whole complex of nature and history is present to the mind of God in the totality. This is surely the significance of the knowledge of "non-duality." It is the knowledge of being in its total presence and actuality without any duality of space and time or separation. To know things in their eternal "ideas" is to know them in their identity in the mind of God, as if all lines were known from a single point, or all colors in the source of light.

We can say, then, that the world comes into being as an expression of the mind of God. In the Word of God, the Logos, that expression is full and final and complete. The Word is a perfect image of the mind of God, in which is reflected the whole being of God, and also every possible participation of a created being in that infinite being. When the world is created, then this reflection is as it were broken up. The rays, which were focussed in the pure, white light of Being, are broken up into different colors, red, orange, green, blue and violet. Each individual person or thing is like a fragment of that light, which reflects a particular color, a particular aspect of the whole. Or to express it in another way, each of us is like a word, which is spoken by God, a word which is part of a sentence, part of a whole, and all these words are gathered into the unity of that word, which God speaks from all eternity. All that I have of being, of reality, comes from God; all that I have of myself is the limitation of my being, I am like an echo of the Word of God, my being is a reflection of his being. God speaks me, therefore I am.

What then is the purpose of God in creation? In the doctrine of Sankara it is difficult to see any real meaning or purpose in creation. *Maya* appears as an inscrutable mystery, which somehow veils the simplicity of the *Brahman* with the appearance of multiplicity. But in the doctrine of Ramanuja, there is a much more satisfactory explanation. Creation is seen as the "play" (*lila*) of God. Though, as we have seen, creation in his view does not come wholly from the will of God, yet it is a true expression of that will; it is a spontaneous and joyous expression of the divine activity. This comes very near to the Christian conception of the motive of creation. Creation is an expression of freedom and joy, it is an overflow of the bliss of God. There is in the divine nature an infinite flow of life and joy, which is the expression of love. As the divine nature eternally expresses itself in a

Word, which is the conscious reflection of its being, so it ceaselessly communicates itself in an act of love which is its self-communication, and the creation is the expression of this spontaneous joy of self-communication. God wills that other beings should share in his own being, knowledge and bliss, and therefore he creates the world. There is no necessity in this act of creation. It arises from the pure goodness of God, the joy of self-giving. It is an overflow of his goodness, an expression of his love.

But this brings us against the problem of evil. If God creates the world out of love and wills that other beings should share in his joy, why is there evil and suffering in the world? Here again we must remember, as when we consider the nature of creation itself, that we are in the sphere of mystery. There is no rational explanation of the problem of evil; it is beyond our human understanding no less than the fact of creation itself. Yet the existence of evil can be made intelligible to some extent. In the first place it is clear that evil can have no proper existence of its own. Everything that is is good; being and goodness are correlative. Evil is a lack of being, a defect of being; it is a privation. A limb that is injured or an organ that is diseased suffer from a defect in their proper nature; though the effects are very positive, the cause is essentially a defect, a lack of something which is due. In the same way moral evil is due to a defect in the will; it is the failure of the will to grasp the good which it desires. Everyone naturally desires what is good; no one ever chooses evil as such; evil is only chosen when it appears as good. Thus evil always has a negative character; it is a defect of being. In this sense there can be no evil in God, since he is the fullness of being without any defect at all.

How then does evil arise? The Christian doctrine is that evil is an effect of free will. God endows his creatures with the power of free choice, the power to discern between good and evil and to act according to this judgment, but freedom in a finite being necessarily implies the power to choose wrong. Man's very being exists in dependence on God; for him happiness depends on his will corresponding with the will of God. If the will fails to correspond, if it turns away from God and allows itself to be attracted by other things, it sets itself against the order of divine providence and suffers as a consequence. Thus all suffering is ultimately due to sin. According to Christian doctrine there is a "sin of the angels," that is of the cosmic powers, by which sin originally entered into the world, and there is a "sin of man," an original sin, by which mankind as a whole turns away from God and loses its original happiness. Original sin is of course a mystery, which cannot be properly understood by the rational mind since it consists precisely in the fact that man has fallen from the state of intuitive wisdom and communication with God into its present state of dependence on sense and reason. It is only in the light of that intuitive wisdom, which transcends reason, that we can have any understanding of the mystery. In the doctrine of Sankara there is, of course, no problem; original sin is simply the state of ignorance, of blindness, by which the mind falls from the pure consciousness of the *Atman* and imagines an unreal world. But in Ramanuja we find a doctrine which is very close to the Christian. He holds that God produces souls which are capable of good and evil and that it depends on their free choice, whether they choose the good and attain to bliss, or whether they choose the evil and involve themselves in misery. But at the same time Ramanuja holds that God is always drawing souls to himself by his grace. "What the Lord aims at," he says, "is ever to increase happiness to the highest degree, and for this end it is essential that he should reprove and reject the infinite intolerable mass of sins which accumulate in the course of endless ages, and thus check the tendency on the part of individuals to transgress his laws."

Thus there is a witness both in the Vedanta and in Christian faith that man was originally created good and that suffering has entered into the world through the sin of man, however mysterious the sources of this sin may be. But we find also both in Hindu and in Christian thought the idea that in order to check the course of evil in the world, God himself "descends" into the world. The doctrine of the *avatara*—the descent of God—goes back in Hinduism to the Bhagavad Gita, where it is said that when righteousness (*dharma*) declines and unrighteousness increases, then the Lord takes birth.[39] According to Ramanuja, the Lord (Isvara) reveals himself as a Savior (*raksaka*) by entering human history to arrest the progress of sin. The number of the *avataras* has varied in Hindu tradition. The earlier texts mention only ten, which is the commonly accepted figure, but the Bhagavata Purana gives forty and declares that they are innumerable. But some of these *avataras* are regarded as only partial manifestations of God; only that of Krishna, it is said, is a complete incarnation. The difference between the Hindu and the Christian idea of incarnation depends on the difference in their view of creation. In the Hindu view all creation is a "manifestation" of God and is not essentially different from God, so that an *avatara* is only a particular "manifestation" of the divine. This explains why there can be "innumerable" *avataras*. At the same time in the Hindu view, as for instance in that of Ramanuja, the world and souls come forth from the *Brahman* from age to age in an endless cycle, and are then reabsorbed in the state of *pralaya*.

But for the Christian there is a creation, which is not simply a "manifestation" of God, but a real creation in the sense which has been explained, which differs in its very nature from God, that is, which has a created being which is essentially different from the being of God. But in addition for the Christian there is only one creation, which takes place once in time and leads through successive stages to a culmination. The incarnation is a unique historical event in this creation by which the course of human history is given its final direction and reveals its ultimate significance. By sin mankind, that is man as a whole, which is represented by Adam, falls from God, that is falls from the divine life to which it is called, and by the incarnation mankind, that is mankind as a whole, represented by Christ, the "second Adam," is redeemed from sin and restored to the divine life.[40] This is the essential drama of human history. We have to conceive that mankind is an organic unity. Human individuals do not exist in isolation but as members of a Body, an organic whole, which develops in time and space towards its final consummation in eternal life. The purpose of creation is that mankind should share in the life, that is the being, knowledge and bliss of God. By sin the growth of mankind towards this goal is upset and the unity of mankind is disrupted. By the incarnation God himself assumes our fallen nature, redeems it from sin and restores it to unity in the divine life.

How then are we to understand the incarnation? The Christian doctrine is expressed by saying that in Christ the divine and the human nature were united in one person. In his Person, that is in his Self, in the ultimate ground of his being, he was God. He

knew himself as the Word of God, the expression
of the mind of the Father. But at the same time he
was conscious of himself as man, having a human
soul and a human body, sharing the limitations of
human nature. If we compare this with the experience of the Hindu seer, a Ramakrishna or a Ramana
Maharshi to take examples from modern times, we
find an essential difference. For the Hindu seer the
experience of God is an experience of "identity" of
pure being in conscious bliss. This is certainly a profound experience, a genuine experience of God, but
it is not the same as the experience of Christ. His
was an experience of identity in relationship. He
does not say, I am the Father—that he could never
say—but "I and the Father are one."[41] It is a unity in
duality, by which he can say, "I am in the Father and
the Father in me,"[42] which is yet based on an identity
of being, by which he can say, "He who sees me, sees
the Father."[43] It is the experience of the Absolute in
personal relationship, and that would seem to be the
distinctive character of the Christian experience of
God. For Christ communicates this experience of
Sonship to his disciples—"to as many as believed in
him, he gave the power to become sons of God"[44]—
and this comes about through the gift of the Spirit,
by which man is raised to share in the life and consciousness of God.

The significance of the incarnation is, then, that
through it mankind is raised to a participation in the

divine consciousness. Christ experienced himself as the Logos, the Word of God, expressing the mind of the Father, and communicating the divine spirit to the world. Christ as Logos is the Self of the universe. "In him," as St. Paul says, "all things were created."[45] Every created thing from an atom to a man is a "word" of God, and in the Logos, the Word of God, all these "words" are held in the unity of the divine consciousness. When, through sin, this unity was disrupted and man fell from the divine life, then the "Word became flesh,"[46] the Logos assumed the life of the universe and the nature of man to himself and restored it to the unity of the divine life and the divine consciousness. Yet we must not suppose that this "descent" of God implies any change in God. To speak of a "descent" of God or God "becoming" man is to use the language of mythology—though there is no harm in doing so, as long as one understands what one is doing. But strictly speaking by the incarnation God does not descend to man but man is raised to God; a human nature is raised to participation in the nature of God, and in so doing raises up mankind with him. But all this takes place in man; God himself does not change. The whole process of creation, sin, redemption, incarnation and final restoration takes place in man and introduces no change into the being of God, to whom the whole process of time remains always present in its totality.

We may look upon the whole creation, therefore, as a process, by which the universe is being led by a gradual evolution through life in nature and consciousness in man to a participation in the divine life and consciousness. This conception of an evolution of the universe towards an "omega point," an ultimate state, in which life and consciousness converge on the plenitude of life and consciousness in God, has been put before us in recent times in the Christian tradition by Teilhard de Chardin and in the Hindu tradition by Sri Aurobindo. These would seem to represent the most profound insights of modern man, working within the tradition of orthodox religion, to penetrate into the ultimate meaning of life. In the Christian view we find in Christ the point at which human consciousness, evolved over an immense period of time from matter and life, enters finally into the divine consciousness. In the resurrection of Christ matter itself is transformed and becomes the vehicle of the divine life. In him the universe thus finds its ultimate meaning as an expression of the mind of God. In him human history finds its culmination and man realizes his destiny as Son of God.

May we not find in this conception of the restoration of mankind, and with mankind of the universe, to unity through participation in the life of God, an example of the convergence of ancient religious tradition and modern thought? In all the great religions we find this conception of an original unity in which man is at one with nature and with God, the supreme reality. It is found in the *Tao* of

Lao Tsu, in the *Buddha*-nature which all men share of Mahayana Buddhism, in the *Atman* of Hindu tradition and in the Universal Man of Islam. In the past it has been customary to look upon this original unity as something realized in the past, from which man has fallen. Today we think rather in terms of the ascent of man towards a unity for which he constantly aspires. Both Sri Aurobindo and Teilhard de Chardin, as we have said, see in evolution of the universe the gradual convergence of matter and life through consciousness in man to the experience of the divine life and consciousness. Modern man has explored the world of matter and life and consciousness with a thoroughness and exactitude which has never been known before. But in doing so he has lost the knowledge of the divine life and consciousness, which alone give any final meaning to life and consciousness in man. It is there that the ancient religious traditions are needed to bring back to mankind that knowledge of the divine life and consciousness, which have been the goal and aspiration of every great religion. But in so doing the different religions have to take account of the knowledge of matter and life and consciousness, which modern science has given us, and so make their message relevant to modern man. The mysteries of God and creation, of sin and redemption, of incarnation and final restoration are no less relevant to human life today than they were in the past. May our comparative study of these doctrines in Hindu and Christian tradition help all of us to realize more deeply their implications in our own lives, and lead us to a closer understanding and a greater unity with one another.

III. THE ULTIMATE STATE OF MAN AND THE UNIVERSE

WHAT IS THE ULTIMATE state of man and the universe? What is the ultimate meaning of life? What is the ultimate nature of reality? These are questions which every religion and philosophy has tried to answer, and modern man is still seeking an answer to them. There are many today who think that the material world which is presented to our senses is the ultimate reality, and man's task is to make this world as satisfactory as possible for human life by scientific control. This view is as widespread in Capitalist as in Communist countries, in the East as in the West and may well be called the dominant philosophy of today. This view is largely a reaction against the idealist view of life, which regards the material world as unreal or at best as a shadow of the world to come and looks for the ultimate reality in an ideal world. This view has been dominant for a long time in both Hinduism and Christianity and may be called the typical religious view of the world. Sri Aurobindo has characterized these two views in his *Life Divine* as the Materialist Denial and the Ascetic Refusal.[47] He sees the Materialist Denial as typical of Western thought and the Ascetic Refusal as typical of Eastern, especially Indian thought. "It is the revolt of spirit against matter," he says, "that for two thousand years, since Buddhism disturbed the balance of the old Aryan world, has dominated the Indian mind." Against these two views Sri Aurobindo sets the integral view of reality, which seeks to do justice both to the truth of material science and the spiritual intuition, which sees the ultimate reality as beyond this world. May it not be that it is at this precise point that Hindu and Christian thought need to meet and to bring to light that ultimate truth which both have been constantly seeking, and which alone can satisfy the need of modern man?

Indian philosophy has never been without a realist element. In the Vedas themselves, as Sri Aurobindo always insisted, there is a firm basis of realism, and this remains in both the Upanishads and the Bhagavad Gita. In the Vedanta there have been three main schools—*Advaita, Visishadvaita* and *Dvaita*—of which the last may appear the most realist, yet if we examine them closely we shall find that there is a firm basis of realism in them all.

Undoubtedly the system which presents the greatest challenge to the realist mind is the *advaita* doctrine of Sankara. At first appearance there seems to be a complete denial of the reality of the material world. The world of multiplicity, we are told, is a "superimposition" on the Absolute being. It is like a conjuror's show or a dream, which disappears when you awake. It has no more reality than the form of a snake which is "superimposed" on a rope. It is simply an illusion.

Yet if we look more deeply into the doctrine of Sankara, we shall find that it is far more profound than it appears. This accounts for the extraordinary hold that it has had over the best minds of India down to the present day, and for the fascination which it exercises even over those who reject it. It is based on the great affirmation of the Upanishads: "all this (world) is *Brahman*"—"Thou art That." Sankara does not deny the reality of this world or of the human subject; what he denies is the ultimate reality of the appearance of this world and of the human person. It is the appearance of the world to the senses and the rational constructions which the human mind raises upon it—all that, in fact, which the materialist and the logical positivist imagine to be real — which Sankara declares to be unreal. The objective world is real and the human subject is real, but their reality is not what it appears. Sankara has seen with extraordinary penetration that the human mind cannot rest on any image presented to the senses or on any thought presented to consciousness. It has to go beyond both image and thought, if it wants to reach the ultimate reality, the ultimate truth, which cannot be thought or imagined.

Now this is the most penetrating intuition of which the mind is capable. It pierces through all appearances, all the projection of the mind and the senses, to the ultimate truth. And this intuition, Sankara maintains—and with him all Hindu tradition—is a matter of experience. When the mind has reached this intuition of reality, of the self, it knows with the certainty of direct experience. It is this quality of lived experience behind Sankara's thought, like that of all the masters of *advaita*, that gives it such extraordinary power. This is not a mere philosophical speculation or the product of religious enthusiasm. It is the experience of the mind itself in the plenitude of self-consciousness, an awareness of being which is nothing but a reflection of being on itself. This explains the fact that this idea of *advaita*, of non-duality, which may appear empty and barren, a mere "nothing," is yet so infinitely fascinating, the source of unending bliss. One can feel in all Sankara's writings this sense of a truth that must be known, of a beatitude, which leaves nothing to be desired. *Advaita* is being, knowledge and bliss, absolute being in absolute consciousness of absolute bliss. It is the term of all human desire.

Once we have realized this, we begin to see Sankara's conception of "maya" in a new light. Sankara does not deny the reality of the sensible world, of this stone, this leaf, this man. He pierces through the appearances of "name and form" to the ultimate reality of the stone, the leaf, the man—to what it is. The illusion consists in imagining that the construction which our senses put upon this world is the ultimate reality. It is like imagining that the appearance of the movement of the sun round the earth is the truth about the universe. But again the constructions which human reason builds on the evidence of the senses are no less unreliable. The whole world of scientific formulas, of stars and galaxies, of molecules and atoms, of protons and electrons, are only symbols, human constructions which hide the ultimate reality. When we pass beyond the limitations both of sense and reason and grasp the reality itself, that is experience reality in direct consciousness, then alone do we see things as they are. This is why Sankara's non-dual being has the plenitude of absolute reality. It appears empty to sense and reason, but it possesses the fullness of being. In it all the reality of stars and galaxies, of atoms and molecules—all the power of the atom—is contained. Everything we experience here in successive stages in space and time is "there" experienced in its fullness. The dispersion of matter in space and time is then known in its integral wholeness, much as though the radii of a circle were to be known from their central point or the colors of the rainbow in the white light of the sun.

It is the same with the human individual.

Sankara sees beyond the outward marks of the individual, his physical characteristics, his psychic structure, his mental consciousness, to the Person, the Self. Just as the body is the outward expression of the soul and the soul is known through the body, so the soul in its turn is the internal expression of the Spirit, the Self, and in this Self the limitation of human individuality is transcended. The Spirit or Self is the point of human self-transcendence. For it is the mystery of human nature that we are made to transcend ourselves. Every growth of knowledge in a human being, the acquisition of language, the knowledge of reason, of science, of mathematics, is a transcendence of the individual self, a step in the acquisition of a common consciousness. As with science, so with art, every work of art is the result of the transcendence of individual limitations and the discovery of a transcendent world, in which human hearts and minds can meet. So finally in morality, to obey the "law of conscience," to follow the path of "duty," to sacrifice oneself for an ideal, is to transcend one's limitations and to experience a new order of reality, which makes us all one with another.

The advaitic experience is simply the culmination of this human experience of transcendence. In advaitic experience we enter the ground of human consciousness, the source of science and art and morality. In this source the principles of science, art and morality are known not in their particular applications, but in their root and ground. The more comprehensive a mind is, the more it is able to hold within the grasp a single idea. It is said that Mozart could apprehend a whole symphony in a single instant in all its parts, just as a mathematician may hold the solution to innumerable practical problems in a single theory. But the experience of *advaita* passes beyond that of the artist or the mathematician. It is the experience of living Truth. It is the very Person, the Spirit, which is experienced in its ground. This means that the human individual finds himself in the community of mankind. If we could know ourselves completely, we should know human nature itself; and knowing human nature, we should know the principle not only of souls but also of bodies, that is, we should know matter in its principle, since the human body is a compendium of the universe, a "microcosm" within the "macrocosm." Thus to know oneself with the intuitive knowledge of "wisdom" or "contemplation" would be to know the universe both of nature and of souls.

We can see this process at work already in a man of genius like Shakespeare or Goethe. Shakespeare knew "human nature" from within by knowing himself with an extraordinary depth and complexity and from this experience of self he was able to create a world of human beings which reflects all the complexities of human nature. Goethe seems to have been seeking for a corresponding "interior" knowledge of nature, to acquire the same kind of intuitive vision of nature as the poet has of man. But these are only imperfect reflections of that whole, integral, entire knowledge of all men and all things "from within" which is the goal of all human knowledge. Is it possible to attain such a kind of knowledge on earth? Hindu tradition affirms that it is—that it is possible to be *jivanmukta*, to attain "liberation" from all spatial and temporal limitations while still on earth. The insight into human nature, even into specific human problems, found in great sages like Ramana Maharshi, would be an example of this kind of transcendent knowledge. Christian tradition has rather held that the perfection of such knowledge is only to be found after death, when the present limitations of the body are transcended.

What then is the relation between Hinduism and Christianity on this most vital question of the advaitic experience? How can this most profound of all the insights of Hinduism be related to Christian doctrine? This is the question to which we would like to attempt an answer. In order to do so, we will take as the norm of Christian doctrine the teaching of St. Thomas Aquinas, the great doctor of the Church in the thirteenth century, who holds much the same place in Catholic tradition as Sankara holds in Hindu. Like Sankara he was a man of profound mystical experience, who yet remained firmly within the orthodox tradition of his faith, and at the same time possessed one of the most perfectly logical minds in human history. Now for St. Thomas, as for Sankara, God is absolutely "without duality."

He is absolutely "simple" in his being, without "composition" of any sort, whether of matter and form, or substance and accident, or of mode or attribute, or even of essence and existence,[48] because there is nothing that can in any way limit or qualify the pure and simple act of his existence. Further St. Thomas holds like Sankara that God is pure intelligence; he is Being in perfect consciousness of itself. He knows all things in the simple act of his mind, in which there is no composition of ideas.[49] St. Thomas declares without hesitation that the "ideas" of things which exist in the mind of God are identical with his essence. In other words, God knows all things in identity with himself. The "idea" in God is the type or exemplar, from which all forms of being on earth are derived, and also the principle, by which all things on earth are known. This means that all things exist in God in their ideas and principles, so that God knows all things down to the minutest particle of their being. Every event in space and time from the beginning to the end of the world is known by God in the one, pure, simple act of his intelligence.

St. Thomas, then, is in agreement with Sankara that the divine nature is absolutely simple "without duality," and that the divine mind, which is simply the consciousness of being, knows all things in an absolute identity with itself. There can be no doubt that Sankara and Aquinas have together reached the most fundamental understanding of the ultimate nature of being and consciousness. Our human experience of being and consciousness compels us to seek for an ultimate ground of being and consciousness in which all duality disappears, and the knower, the thing known and the act of knowing are all one. But we can now carry this parallel a step further. Sankara holds that the human mind only realizes its true nature, when it has the actual experience of this identity, when it knows itself in an act in which it is identified with being. Now there is a tradition in the Church, which goes back to the Greek Fathers, that the ultimate destiny of man is to know himself in the "idea," by which he eternally exists in the mind of God. Indeed, as we shall see, the ultimate destiny of the universe is to return to its "idea" in the mind of God. Man, and with him the universe, of which he is the integrating form, has "fallen" from the state of divine consciousness for which he was created and become subject to the laws of space and time. By the incarnation of the Logos, all these "ideas" or "words" (*logoi*), which have become separated from the Word, are reunited with their Principle. This view of the Greek Fathers was taken up by Aquinas and the other doctors of the Middle Ages with certain refinements and it remains the fundamental framework of Christian doctrine on this subject.[50]

Thus we find that Christian doctrine holds with Sankara that the ultimate end of man is to "participate in the divine nature," to share in God's own mode of consciousness, and hence to know himself and all things in their identity in the divine essence.

We are justified therefore in saying that there is a Christian tradition of the ultimate state of man and the universe, which is identical with that of Sankara. God himself is "without duality," his knowledge or consciousness is "without duality," and the end of man is to participate in this "non-dual" mode of being and consciousness in God. But does this mean that there is no difference between man and God? This is the crucial question, which we have to answer. Sankara felt obliged to hold that if God, or the *Brahman*, is the absolute being, there can be no other being beside him; the appearance of a world of distinct beings and distinct persons is an illusion, a "superimposition" on the being of God. Is there any way of avoiding this conclusion while maintaining the absolutely non-dual being of God? We believe that there is. We agree with Sankara that it is impossible to admit with Ramanuja that the being of God is qualified in any way by the world, or to say with Madhva that the world is eternally distinct from God, though dependent on him. The Christian doctrine of creation, as we have seen, maintains that the world does not add anything to the being of God or take anything away. God alone is being, and nothing else "exists" in the same way as God exists. But the world can be said to exist as an "image" of God, a reflection of his being.

In order to understand this, we must remind ourselves that the world derives its whole being from God. The actuality of anything that exists derives from the pure actuality of God. The world has nothing of itself at all. What distinguishes the world from God is its "not-being," its lack of being, its limitation. The "idea" which exists in the plenitude of being in God in identity with him is given a limited existence in itself. The absolute is reflected in the relative, the infinite in the finite, the eternal in the temporal. Thus the world considered in itself, apart from God, is strictly nothing, it has no being at all. It is a pure illusion, and this is the deep truth underlying Sankara's conception of "maya." But according to Christian belief God can give a relative being to the world, a being whose reality comes wholly from God and whose unreality, or lack of being, comes from the limitation of the creature. This can be expressed in another way by saying that the world has in itself a potential being, but no actual being. The concept of "potency" was introduced into philosophy by Aristotle, as an answer to the problem posed by Parmenides and Heraclitus in regard to "being," and "becoming," and is one of the most profound concepts of his philosophy. It was taken over by St. Thomas Aquinas and made one of the key concepts of his theology. A stone or a piece of wood, according to Aristotle, has the "power" or "potency" to become a statue. This is a "passive" potency, a potency which it cannot realize itself, but which can be realized by a sculptor, who gives "form" or actuality to this potency.

From this Aristotle derived the idea that the "matter" of the universe, the principle of limitation, of inertia, of not-being, is a pure potentiality of being, which has no actuality. It has no existence in itself, but receives existence from another. This is what he called "first matter," the basic principle of matter in the universe. Matter, as we know it, is not pure potency, it is composed of act and potency; it is a potency which has been actualized by receiving a "form," atomic or molecular, or whatever it may be. As matter is the principle of limitation, of not-being, so "form" is the principle of being, of actuality. In the philosophy of St. Thomas these forms in nature, which constitute the structure of the universe, are reflections of the eternal "ideas" in the mind of God. Thus God who is pure being, pure actuality, brings the world into being by giving "form" or actuality to matter, which in itself is the pure potentiality of being. Can we see from this how the world has a real being, which is wholly derived from God, which is simply a reflection of the being of God, while in itself it has a mere potentiality of being, a kind of "not being," which limits its being and distinguishes it from God? Would not this principle of "potentiality" correspond very closely to the "maya" of Sankara?

Thus we can conceive creation taking place in God in the eternal decree, by which he eternally wills the existence of beings, who shall participate in his own being and share in his consciousness and bliss. Then by a free act of his will, which yet introduces no change whatsoever in him, by the delight of self-giving, which eternally exists in his Spirit, he causes the existence of beings other than himself, which are like the reflection of his own being in the "potency" of matter. Thus without losing his character of absolute independence, without ceasing to be absolutely simple and unchanging, God wills the existence of a universe, which is a reflection of his being, which is capable of sharing in his consciousness and participating in his bliss. The evolution of the world is the gradual ascent of being from the bare potentiality of "first matter" through the various forms of inorganic being, then of living matter through the various forms of plant and animal, until in man being becomes conscious of itself. The evolution of man is a gradual ascent through different forms of consciousness, of science, art and morality until he begins to realize the divine consciousness which is the ultimate goal of the evolutionary process. But in this process, as we have seen, there is an element of "sin," of disorder, a failure to correspond with the evolutionary intention of nature. Thus there is one movement in nature, which is carrying all things and all men towards God and eternal life, and there is another movement, which is drawing things back to lower forms of life and eventually back to the original "chaos," the negation of being.

Now this movement affects the whole creation. According to Aquinas all creatures have a natural desire for God, for being, which derives from the basic capacity for being which is in the first matter. There is a force in nature, which is continually moving all creatures towards a greater fulfillment of being. Teilhard de Chardin has shown how this force working in evolution gradually evolves more and more complex forms of being, from inanimate matter to man, and at the same time develops a more and more profound unity "within," which becomes conscious in man. We can say, therefore, that the desire for consciousness is implicit in matter from the beginning. Consciousness is simply the evolution of that principle of "form" or actuality which is present in nature from the beginning, and which derives from the principle of pure actuality, which is also pure consciousness, in God. The whole universe is thus being continually drawn by the principles inherent in its being back to its origin in God.

Can we begin to see from this how matter has its place in the whole plan of the universe and in the evolution of man? In Indian thought, as Sri Aurobindo remarked, there has been a "revolt of spirit against "matter"; and the tendency has been to see the destiny of man in terms of a "release" from material being. In the ultimate state, according to Sankara there is no place for matter; there is nothing but pure consciousness, which is the state of pure spirit. In the philosophy of Ramanuja also the soul is essentially a spiritual being, which finds its happiness in the contemplation of God. The body is like a suit of clothes or, as he says, like dust on a diamond, which hides the pure spirituality of the soul, and has eventually to be shed. But in the Christian view the soul and body together make up the human person. The soul grows into consciousness through the body, experiences itself through the body, and seeks always to penetrate the body with its consciousness. The aim of evolution is, therefore, not to separate soul and body, but to render the body—and hence matter as a whole—more and more open to the influence of the soul, that is of consciousness, so that eventually the body is transfigured, and becomes the pure expression of the spirit. It is the great merit among Indian thinkers of Sri Aurobindo to have realized the full significance of matter in the ascent of evolution and to have given it its proper place in the plan of creation.

In the Christian conception the place of matter in the ultimate state of man is revealed in the doctrine of the resurrection of the body. This must not be understood in a crude sense, as though man will rise again with his present body in his present mode of consciousness. As matter has been gradually transformed, so as to become the vehicle of life and consciousness, so it is destined to be finally transformed, so that it transcends its present limitations and becomes the vehicle of the divine consciousness. Such a "spiritual body" cannot be properly conceived, since it would transcend the present condition of space and time and would be the expression of a different mode of consciousness from our present mode. In that state the human consciousness would transcend both sense and reason and know everything intuitively from within. The world of matter, which we know externally through our senses, would then be known internally, just as to some extent we now know our own bodies. But in that state the body, and with it the whole material universe, would be completely translucent, a pure expression of the inner life of the Spirit.

There is much in this conception of the ultimate state of man and the universe, which can be paralleled in the Vedanta, especially in the Vaishnavite tradition. That the enjoyment of the divine being, consciousness and bliss is the end of man and the universe is the accepted view of the whole tradition of the Vedanta, and this alone constitutes one of the glories of Indian thought, that it has realized so universally and so completely what is the ultimate end and purpose of life. In the view of Sankara there is, of course, properly speaking no end to be attained. The divine being, consciousness and bliss is the one, unchanging reality, and wisdom consists in the realization of that which always "is" and can never cease to be. In the doctrine of Ramanuja there is something much closer to the Christian view. He holds, as we have seen, that the soul has fallen from its original state of blissful contemplation of the Godhead and become connected with a material body. Matter and the body are simply the conditions under which the soul is enabled to realize its true nature of a pure spirit, and to return to its original state, in which it knows itself as an eternal mode of the divine being and enjoys the intuitive vision of God as the highest Self. This conception of the soul as really distinct from God and yet sharing in the consciousness of God and enjoying the bliss of perfect communion with him, comes very close to the Christian view. But Ramanuja finds no place for the body in this final state. The soul can enjoy the contemplation of the universe in God, but it has no longer need of a body.

In Vallabha, however, another Vaishnavite doctor, we find a most interesting development of the concept of the ultimate nature of reality. His is surely one of the most remarkable of the different systems of the Vedanta.[51] While Sankara in his system of *advaita* maintained that the *Brahman* alone exists and the multiplicity of the world is "superimposed" on the one being of God, Vallabha held that God and the universe are essentially the same. There is no real difference between them. This system he called *suddhadvaita* or pure *advaita*. According to this theory God himself is being, knowledge and bliss in its absolute plenitude and perfection. In unconscious nature God, the *Brahman*, appears as being, but his knowledge and bliss are hidden. In man God appears as being and consciousness, but his bliss is hidden. Finally, God himself as the fullness of being, knowledge and bliss dwells both in unconscious nature and in the soul as the *antaryamin*, the inner Witness or Ruler. *Maya*, according to Vallabha, is the illusion which is created by the soul in turning away from God, so that it sees nature and souls apart from

God, not as they really are, as partial manifestation of his being.

Thus everything in nature is to be seen properly as a form of God. As different pots made out of common clay are simply different forms of clay, so all the different forms of nature are different forms of God. This image of the pot and the clay goes back to the Upanishads, but Vallabha interprets it in his own way. He has the beautiful idea that in nature God, as it were, puts himself at the disposal of man. A pot, for instance, is a form of God, in which he makes himself a means to get water, a cow is a form in which he gives milk to man, and so through all the forms of nature. God, he says, is the *dharmin*, and the forms of nature are the *dharmas*. This means that all the forms of nature are "hidden" in God and are one with him. Creation is simply God's self-manifestation, by which he manifests himself, now in this form, now in that, but the whole deity is really contained in every form.

There is much in the system of Vallabha which is deeply impressive and attractive to a Christian. He finds there the conception of a personal God, whose nature is being, knowledge and bliss, but who is also love itself; a God who created the world, that is who manifests himself in the world, in the sheer delight of self-giving and gives himself in love to those who give themselves to him. In this view the beatitude of the soul consists in a total abandonment to God by which it is transformed into the likeness of God and knows itself as existing in and through and for God. All this is in profound accord with Christian thought, and only shows again how the same spirit of God has been at work in India as in the West, leading them by different ways to the knowledge of the mystery of his being, of his grace and of his love. The doctrine of grace is particularly remarkable in Vallabha, because there we find the conception of a total abandonment to God, so that God acts entirely in the soul and the soul knows itself not as partly but as wholly moved by God.

Yet with all this it can hardly be denied that the system of Vallabha is essentially pantheistic. It is, of course, not a crude pantheism, but a system of the utmost subtlety and refinement; it is one of the masterpieces of religious thought. Yet the element of pantheism remains. Ramanuja had tried to save the independence of God by saying that nature and souls are modes of the divine being, which do not affect the divine essence. Vallabha maintains that the universe is simply a manifestation of different aspects of the divine being, in all of which God is equally present. In other words he maintains that the universe is a transformation of God, but a transformation in which the divine nature does not really undergo a change, but simply reveals certain aspects of its being while concealing others. This world which Vallabha describes has a certain resemblance to the "world of ideas" in Christian thought, which is simply the divine nature itself conceived under the different aspects of being which are implicit in it. If Vallabha had said that the world is the divine nature conceived under different aspects so that it appears now as unconscious nature, now as conscious being in man, he would have been nearer to the truth; but he seems to have held to a real transformation in the being of God, which it is difficult to accept. Yet his theory remains of great interest.

There is a hint in his doctrine of the Christian conception of the world of the resurrection; the "new creation,"[52] as St. Paul calls it. For Vallabha holds that the world as we see it, subject to change and decay, is really a world of illusion, because it is the world seen in separation from God. If we could see the world, as it is, we should see it simply as an expression of the divine being in its different aspects, making explicit that multiplicity of being, which is implicit in the divine unity. Now in the Christian view of the "new creation," it is held that matter itself will be transformed so as to be the outward expression of the divine consciousness, just as the human body is now the outward expression of the human consciousness. In other words, in the resurrection the material universe, and with it the human body, will become a "manifestation" of the divine life and consciousness; matter will be wholly transformed by spirit and manifest all the different aspects of the being of God. There is thus a profound truth underlying Vallabha's theory. Yet we cannot accept it as it stands. We have to say that the divine nature itself cannot undergo any change or transformation; it remains ever the same in the fullness of its perfection of being. But we can say that God can take up nature and man by a free act of his grace, so as to share in his own life and knowledge and bliss.

Thus we come back to what is perhaps the fundamental difference between the Hindu and the Christian point of view. For the Hindu, except in the system of Madhva (and it may be added the Saiva Siddhanta) the universe is essentially of the same nature as God, and the end of man is to realize his essential oneness with God and so to enjoy forever the divine life and bliss. In the system of Madhva, as we have seen, there is a real difference between God and man and nature, and the ultimate state of man and the universe is that in which man knows himself in his radical dependence on God and finds his joy in the contemplation of the divine beauty, while remaining ever separated from it. It might be thought that this is nearer to the Christian view, but in fact it is not so. The Christian doctrine of divine grace goes beyond Madhva and brings us nearer to Ramanuja and to Vallabha. For according to Christian doctrine, though man and nature are created really distinct and different from God, yet by a free act of grace God communicates to them a participation in his own nature. The soul by grace participates in the divine being, knowledge and bliss. It exists no longer merely in its own separate nature but in the nature of God himself. It knows not merely by its own mode of rational knowledge, but by the divine mode of consciousness. Its bliss is not simply the beatitude of a soul that has reached the fulfillment of its natural desires, but that of a soul that has transcended its own mode of being and shares in the very bliss of God, that is in the plenitude of the divine love.

It can be seen how close this comes to the view of Ramanuja and Vallabha and of the whole Hindu tradition, yet a difference remains. A Christian will never say that the soul is of the same essence as God. He will never use the analogy of the pot and the clay or of sparks coming from a fire or of a drop of water mingling with the ocean. All these images imply a sameness of essence. The Christian mystics speak rather of iron which is heated by the fire, so that it becomes red-hot and is wholly penetrated by the fire, so as to be transformed by it and yet remains iron and does not actually become fire. Or again they compare the soul to air, which is wholly filled with light and manifests the light, but yet does not become light. Thus the difference in nature between the soul and God always remains. The soul participates in the divine nature, but it is not God. It participates in the divine mode of consciousness, but it does not comprehend God. It participates in the divine bliss and is so united to God that it loves him with the very love by which God himself loves, yet still the soul and God are not the same.

If the soul is thus transformed by participation in the divine nature, so also must the body be, and with the body the whole material universe. We have seen how close this comes to Vallabha's conception of the world as a manifestation of God. But there is also a remarkable resemblance with Ramanuja's doctrine of the world as the body of God. According to Christian doctrine God in Christ assumes the nature of man into the divine life, so that mankind, renewed by divine grace, becomes what St. Paul calls the "body of Christ":[53] that is it becomes an organic whole in which the principle of life is the divine life itself, communicated to it through the humanity of Christ. This transformation of man by the divine life begins even now on earth, but it is only completed when man's body is also transformed by the resurrection. But when this takes place, then the whole universe is transformed together with the body of man. In this sense the whole universe then becomes the "body" of Christ. It is one and the same principle of life, the divine life itself, which animates the whole creation. Then man and nature will become wholly penetrated by the divine consciousness and share alike in the bliss of the divine love, which is poured out on the whole creation. Then we can say that the whole universe "of insentient and sentient beings" will become the "body" of God.

Thus we can see how much there is in common between the Hindu and the Christian view of the ultimate state of man and the universe. Both alike see the ultimate end of man in the enjoyment of the divine being, knowledge and bliss, but in their interpretation of the exact relation between man and nature and God in this final state, there is a difference between different schools of the Vedanta and between Hindu and Christian thought. Yet may we not see a kind of convergence in these different lines of thought? May we not see here an indication of the lines upon which there might be a meeting of Hindu and Christian thought? A Christian cannot but feel a deep sympathy with the different systems of Vaishnavite faith with their wonderful conception of infinite eternal and transcendent Being, who is yet a personal God, free from every taint of sin and imperfection, who seeks to deliver man from sin and to communicate to him his own grace and love. But if the Vaishnavite faith has much to attract us, it is yet to Sankara that we must turn for the most profound conception of the ultimate state of man and the universe. For when we say that man will share in the divine mode of being and consciousness, we mean that man will share in the "non-dual" being and consciousness of God. According to Christian tradition in the beatific vision man will know himself and all things in their "ideas" in God, and this, as we have seen, means that man will know himself in "identity" with God. As God sees all things and all men as reflections of his own being, as partial and limited expressions of his own perfect and infinite being, so in the beatific vision man will see himself and all things as expressions of the mind of God. He will see all things and all men in the Word, that is in Christ, who takes up the whole creation and the whole of humanity into the life and light of God. All things will then be reunited in God, wholly penetrated by the light of God, forming a single image of God.

But this means that all differences, as we know them, will disappear. Here we begin to see the full significance of Sankara's *advaita*. In God all differences which appear in nature and all distinctions known to the human mind are transcended. To share in the vision of God means therefore that we have to pass beyond all concepts of the rational mind and all images derived from the sense. We must pass into that world of non-duality, in which our present mode of consciousness is transcended. We must pass into that "divine darkness" of which Dionysius speaks, which appears dark only because it is pure light; we must ascend to that state of "unknowing," in which all human knowledge fades away, and we shall at last know truly "even as we are known." In this view of the ultimate mystery of being, which is the beginning and the end of all our human aspiration, Hindu and Christian unite not only with one another but also with the Buddhist and the Muslim.

There is a final transcendent state of being and consciousness, in which alone perfect bliss is to be found, to which every great religion bears witness. This state transcends all concepts of the mind and images of the sense and is known only when the divine being chooses to reveal himself to man. This is the ultimate mystery, the ultimate truth, to which everything in nature aspires, but which so transcends the whole order of nature that it appears as darkness rather than light, as something unreal and illusory, as a Void, a Silence, a Negation of Being. And yet such is the witness of every great religious tradition, in this Void, in this Darkness, in this Silence, all fullness, all light, all truth, all goodness, all love, all joy, all peace, all happiness is to be found. May our study of different traditions of religion lead us all to a deeper understanding of this divine mystery and to a share in a greater measure of this divine bliss!

ENDNOTES

FOREWORD

1. *Introduction to The Upanishads: Translated for the Modern Reader* by Ecknath Easwaran, (Tamales: Nilgiri Press, 1987), 13.
2. Bede Griffiths, *Marriage of East and West* (Springfield: Templegate, 1982), 68.
3. Raimon Panikkar, *Christophany: The Fullness of Man*, trans. Alfred DiLascia (Maryknoll, NY: Orbis Books, 2004), 185.
4. Bruno Barnhart, *The Future of Wisdom* (New York: Continuum, 2007/Rhinebeck, NY: Monkfish Book Publishing Company, 2018), 56.
5. Griffiths, *Marriage of East and West*, 68.

I. THE MYSTERY OF THE GODHEAD

6. *cf.* Brihadaranyaka Upanishad. 3.6 & 7.
7. Chandogya Upanishad. 6.12.
8. Br. Up. 2.3.6.
9. Mandukya Up. 7.
10. Kat ha Up. 2.6.12.
11. Br. Up. 2.4.13.

[12] Br. Up. 4.3.21.
[13] Br. Up. 2.4.5.
[14] John. 1.18.
[15] 1 Timothy. 6.16.
[16] 1 Timothy. 1.17.
[17] *Stromata.* 5.12.
[18] *De Principiis.* 1.1.5.
[19] *On the Divine Names.* 1.5.
[20] *ibid.* 1.7.
[21] *ibid.* 1.4.
[22] *On the Life of Moses.*
[23] John. 1.1.
[24] John. 1.4.
[25] John. 1.3.
[26] Wisdom of Solomon. 7.26.
[27] Wisdom of Solomon. 7.27.
[28] Wisdom of Solomon. 8.1.
[29] Hebrews. 1.3.
[30] 2 Peter. 1.4.
[31] Mystical Theology. 1.

II. CREATION AND INCARNATION

[32] Isa Upanishad. Invocation.
[33] *Commentary on the Brahma Sutras.* 4.4.22.
[34] *ibid.* 1.1.9.
[35] *ibid.* 1.4.27.
[36] *Commentary on the Bhagavad Gita.* 10.10.11.
[37] For Madhava's teachings *cf. Madhva's Teachings in His Own Words*, B.N.K. Sharma.
[38] Genesis. 1.1.
[39] Bhagavad Gita. 4.7.

40 *cf.* 1 Corinthians. 15.22.
41 John. 10.30.
42 John. 14.10.
43 John. 14.9.
44 John. 1.12.
45 Colossians. 1.16.
46 John. 1.14.

III. THE ULTIMATE STATE OF MAN
AND THE UNIVERSE

47 *The Life Divine.* Vol. 1, ch. 2 and 3.
48 *Summa Theologica.* I.iii.1-8.
49 *ibid.* I.xv.
50 *cf. Christian Philosophy in the Middle Ages* by Etienne Gilson.
51 I am indebted for this view of the philosophy of Vallabha to Johanns, *Through Christ to the Vedanta,* published in The Light of the East.
52 2 Corinthians. 5.17.
53 Ephesians. 1.23.

Bede Griffiths was a Benedictine monk who achieved worldwide recognition for his pioneering efforts to bridge the great traditions of Christian and Hindu faith. He advocated a global spiritual friendship, rather than a global religion, cultivating respect for each other's spiritual practices. He died in 1993 at the age of 84. He was a pioneer in the Hindu-Christian interfaith dialogue. He was a life-long friend of C. S. Lewis.